REALITY IS
ALL THE GOD
THERE IS

*Avatar Adi Da Samraj in a formal occasion of
granting His blessing to His devotees*

REALITY IS
ALL THE GOD
THERE IS

The Single Transcendental Truth
Taught by the Great Sages
and the Revelation of Reality Itself

Avatar Adi Da Samraj

Inner Traditions
Rochester, Vermont

Inner Traditions
One Park Street
Rochester, Vermont 05767
www.InnerTraditions.com

Originally published under the title *The Ancient Reality-Teachings* by the Dawn Horse Press,
Middletown, California

Library of Congress Cataloging-in-Publication Data
Adi Da Samraj, 1939–
   Reality is all the God there is : the single transcendental truth taught by the great sages and
the revelation of reality itself / Avatar Adi Da Samraj.
      p. cm.
   Rev. ed. of: The ancient reality-teachings.
   Includes bibliographical references (p.   ) and index.
   ISBN 978-1-59477-257-3 (pbk.)
   1. Spiritual life—Adidam (Organization). 2. Buddhism. 3. Advaita. I. Adi Da Samraj,
1939– Ancient reality-teachings. II. Title.
   BP610.B81126 2008
   299'.93—dc22

                                                                              2008025225

Printed and bound in the United States by Lake Book Manufacturing

10 9 8 7 6 5 4 3 2 1

Text design by Diana April and layout by Jon Desautels
This book was typeset in Garamond Premier Pro with ITC Galliard as the display typeface

CONTENTS

CONVENTIONS

A Note about Avatar Adi Da's Writings

The writings of Adi Da Samraj employ conventions of capitalization, punctuation, and underlining that differ in various ways from standards commonly applied in written American English. Certain terms are also employed with a very specific meaning, which is often indicated by the use of quote marks around the term. Many of these terms and the explanations of their specific usage can be found in the glossary provided at the end of the book.

These unique conventions, which sometimes vary even within the separate sections of a text, are an intrinsic part of Adi Da's writings. They have been developed by him to support his revelation that it is the dualistic and separative point of view of the ego that prevents the realization of Reality—a point of view that is also the basis for ordinary speech and written language.

Adi Da Samraj writes, "The conventions of everyday speech and writing are based on a social convention that is, in Reality Itself, untrue. The 'I' of the presumed separate and independent 'self' is an illusory (or, in Reality Itself, non-existing) and abstract . . . identity, by which . . . all common spoken and written language is proposed." His writing, he says, "is <u>not</u> spoken or communicated from—or, Ultimately, even to— the egoic 'point of view'." Therefore, he says, a "unique convention" was developed for his writing that is a visual representation or "picture" of a form of speech that is not based on egoity.

It is the intent of Adi Da that this form of writing will enable you to be "Released from having to exercise the egoic vision and its separate and separative 'point of view.'" The unusual conventions, he writes, "interrupt the common flow of mind, and Signal the Heart of 'you' that <u>this</u> moment <u>Is</u> The Necessary Instant of Self-Awakening—to <u>Be</u> <u>As</u> 'you' <u>Are</u>."

Additionally, the introduction to this book is by a formal devotee of Avatar Adi Da who uses capitalized pronouns and other signs of respect for Adi Da in her writing, in addition to observing similar conventions as those found in the rest of the text.

INTRODUCTION

❖

Carolyn Lee, PhD

From time to time in human history, Great Sages have appeared who have, to one degree or another, agreed to instruct devotees. However, they do not teach from the position of an "I" speaking to "you" or "me". A truly Great Sage speaks as the very condition, the Radiant Ocean of Being, That *is* Reality. Adi Da Samraj, from the beginning of His lifetime, has shown the signs of being such a one. He is here, in the brief span of a human lifetime, to show that the Ultimate Reality and Truth is not, as He has remarked, a "blank absolute", nor is it a "Creator-God", making the world and implicated in the human drama. Rather, the Very One Who *Is,* is by Nature moved to Liberate—to set beings free of identification with the sticky web of illusions that makes up our usual life. The Reality-Teaching of Avatar Adi Da Samraj is a great gift to all who need to understand human life from the viewpoint of Ultimate Truth, beyond the winds of doctrine and the competing philosophies that have made and unmade the cultures of humankind.

The content of this book—which came into being with astonishing speed at the end of 2005 and the beginning of 2006—originated when Adi Da Samraj was moved to make His own rendering or "interpretive translation" of *The Heart of the Ribhu Gita,* a text in the Advaitic ("non-dual") tradition of Transcendental Wisdom. He did this in order to elucidate, and thereby honor, its full meaning. His intent was to draw out the real intention of Ribhu (the Sage who generated it), as only another Realizer of Truth can. Having completed the work, Avatar Adi Da read the text to His devotees in a live internet occasion, during which He commented upon it further.

In the following weeks, Adi Da Samraj went on to render other principal texts from the traditions of the Great Sages in a similar manner. By "Sage", He means one who is focused in the Knowledge of Reality at the root, Realizing What *Is*. Adi Da Samraj gave His attention to other great texts from the tradition of Advaita Vedanta as well as from the Buddhist tradition, including selections from the early Buddhist scriptures of the Pali Canon, a work attributed to the early Buddhist philosopher Nagarjuna, works attributed to the eighth-century Sage Shankara, who systematized the teachings of the Upanishads into what became the Advaitic tradition of Vedanta, and a text known as the *Devikalottara*. In each case, He brought the essence of the instruction to the fore, with an elegant and illumined understanding. Texts whose meanings were only partially (or cryptically) expressed even in the original—let alone in translation—suddenly shone forth, like rough gems cut by an expert hand. *Reality Is All The God There Is* presents these masterful "translations", together with Adi Da's discourses about the traditional texts and about His own Reality-Teaching.*

The traditional teachings rendered here by Adi Da Samraj were originally transmitted orally, even over long stretches of time, before they were written down. Little reliable historical information about the Great Sages whose teachings gave rise to these texts is available, and the original circumstances in which the teachings were transmitted have faded into the mists of time. We do know that the general context was that of the

---

*The texts in *Reality Is All The God There Is* are drawn from a larger (unpublished) text by Adi Da Samraj entitled *The Gnosticon*. *The Gnosticon* presents a broader array of texts to illuminate the Buddhist and Advaitic traditions of transcendental (or non-dual) "Gnosis" and to further clarify the unique transcendental/spiritual nature of the "Gnosis" embodied in Avatar Adi Da's own Reality-Teachings.

Upanishadic tradition of India, which goes back thousands of years. In that tradition a seeker would approach a Realizer in the forest, or some secluded place, hoping that he or she might consent to impart a teaching. Such teachings would then be duly remembered and passed on.

At the same time, as Avatar Adi Da points out in this book, the forest hermitage was not the only place of instruction. There was also an ancient tradition of dharmic debate between teachers of different schools—often taking place in the presence of a ruler and his court.

Whatever the life context of these great teachings, today we confront them primarily as literary artifacts. Their origins are inaccessible. While the words of the Masters continue in some form, the Masters themselves, and their living play of instruction, have disappeared. From the divorce of the teacher from the teaching—which inevitably tends to occur over time—have sprung endless revisions, dilutions, and distortions of the original wisdom. The story of the Sage Ribhu and his devotee Nidagha, which is told in this book [chapter XI], is a parable that reveals the truth that there is no direct Realization of Reality apart from the relationship to the Master and his or her spiritual help and skillful means.

The original wisdom of the traditional teachings is now revealed through the immense Grace of the living presence, in our time, of Avatar Adi Da Samraj, whose own Reality-Teachings have arisen in a contemporary "Upanishadic" circumstance—the situation of devotees gathered at His Feet in one of His Hermitage Sanctuaries.

THE HIDDEN STRUCTURE OF THE BODY-MIND

The entirety of religion, according to Adi Da Samraj, can be seen as basically the attempt, in all its variant forms, to console, "save", transform, or even dissolve the apparent "I"—which we all presume we are. He goes further, adding the extraordinary insight that the kind of religion (or even rejection of religion) that we settle for depends on the dimension of the "I" with which we identify.

In the ancient Oriental view, the "I" is more than the body, and more than merely "body and soul". Rather, the human being is a complex psycho-physical structure composed of a hierarchy of layers or sheaths.[1] In the simplest understanding, this esoteric anatomy is composed of three fundamental dimensions—which Adi Da Samraj defines as "gross, subtle, and causal", or "outer, inner, and root".[2]

> The gross (or outer) dimension corresponds to the physical level of experience and the waking state.
>
> The subtle (or inner) dimension is comprised of everything related to mind, emotion, and energy, including the domain of dreaming and psychic experience, as well as the range of supernormal experience that is commonly called "mystical".
>
> The causal (or root) dimension refers to the depth where the sense of the "I" and the "other" originates, thereby "causing", or generating, the worlds of subtle and gross experience that extend from that root-presumption of separate "identity".

According to Adi Da Samraj, popular, or *exoteric,* religion is strictly an outer, waking-state affair, motivated by the concerns of physical existence. Whatever its particular characteristics of doctrine and practice in any time and place, exoteric religion is a search for consolation and salvation through belief in some kind of "Creator-God" or patron-deity, and through adherence to a moral code of behavior that promotes social order.

The *esoteric* traditions, accounting for a small minority of humanity's religious endeavors, conduct a more refined and inward form of seeking. They aspire to transcend the common myths and awaken directly to what is Ultimate. They all speak, in one way or another, of Realizing an Ultimate Source-Condition of the impermanent, arising world. But this intention has various meanings and implications, depending on the orientation of the particular tradition. There is not only a fundamental difference between the exoteric religions and the esoteric traditions, but there are real differences between the esoteric schools themselves.

Avatar Adi Da's revelation, evident throughout His writings, is that these differences correspond with the esoteric anatomy just described (with its gross, subtle, and causal dimensions). Esoteric practitioners focus either in the subtle dimension, which is the realm of the various mystical and Yogic traditions, or in the causal dimension, which is the domain of the Sages, the Realizers who are exclusively invested in knowing the Transcendental Reality. Thus the esoteric traditions of humankind have been polarized around these two different orientations: the orientation to subtle Energy and Light as the means and nature of Realization, on the one hand, and the urge to Realize Consciousness, independent of objects, on the other.

One of Avatar Adi Da's essential communications about Reality—the seven stages of life—is of greatest use to our global human culture. These stages (summarized in the appendix) constitute a fully-developed "map" of the progressive developmental potential of the human being. His paradigm of the progressive stages of life represents an esoteric science that is highly detailed and extremely precise.

In this paradigm, the first three stages of life constitute the ordinary course of human adaptation: bodily, emotional, and mental growth. A great shift has to occur before the ordinary human being—still struggling to adapt in the three foundation stages of psycho-physical development—can take the leap into the fourth stage of life, characterized by a life of devotional communion with the Divine Spirit (however the Divine is conceived or experienced).

In terms of the underlying structure of the gross, subtle, and causal dimensions, the transition to the fourth stage of life is the most critical, because it represents the first entry into the domain of that which is beyond the physical. The fourth stage of life is a bridge between the gross and the subtle. It involves an opening of the body-mind to the dimension of Spiritual Energy, which transforms the beliefs and observances of merely exoteric religion into a real heart practice and potential mystical experience.

In the fifth stage of life the fundamental point of view is no longer that of the waking state, but, rather, a persistent concentration in the subtle energy centers in and above the head, in order to enter into states of ascended bliss—possibly including the experience of subtle lights, visions, sounds, and tastes.

The sixth stage of life goes to the causal root. The effort of sixth stage practitioners is to abide as the Formless Reality (or Consciousness) that is intuited in the depth of meditative contemplation, and to discount or turn away from all experience, in order to find and stay in touch with that Root-Reality.

The various stages of life are illustrated not only in the case of the individual, but also in the cultural evidence of history. Adi Da Samraj refers to the vast and varied process of humanity's wisdom search as the "Great Tradition", and explains how it can be understood in terms of six stages of life—with the potential for the Realization of the seventh (or most ultimate) stage of life.

It is Adi Da's unique revelation that, in the seventh stage of life, Reality is Self-Revealed as both Consciousness *and* Energy, or Conscious Light—the "Bright".[3] This Realization—which resolves what could be called the traditional esoteric "argument" between the "Consciousness point of view" and the "Energy point of view"—is Non-conditional, requiring no effort or intention to maintain. In the words of Adi Da Samraj, it is the "Perfect Knowledge" of Reality.

The Necessity to Prepare for the Ultimate Practice

In preparing the renderings in this book, Adi Da Samraj chose only texts of the sixth-stage type. This is not because He regards the texts and practices of the fourth and fifth stages of life—or even a true culture of the first three stages of life—to be necessarily false. In fact, the point that He makes in all His commentaries on the Great Tradition is that the first six stages of life, and the life-practices associated with each of those stages, represent the full course of human growth that has traditionally been possible. As Adi Da has discussed at great length (in this book and in many others of His books), the seventh (and culminating) stage of life is an entirely new possibility, brought into the conditional domain by His Avataric Appearance here.

Clearly, a preparatory process of growth must be embraced by those who aspire to practice the Ultimate Teaching. Just as an infant cannot suddenly decide to become an adult, a student cannot merely start presuming the Ultimate Position described by the Reality-Teachings in this book. This point is made in all the traditional texts rendered here, and by Adi Da Samraj Himself. One morning, while discussing various scholarly issues relating to the traditional texts, Adi Da Samraj made this point:

> *The Work I have done in this book is an effort to make the traditions speak plain, completely apart from all other kinds of concerns, including scholarly conventions and purposes. This book is about approaching these texts entirely on the presumption that Truth is the matter of importance—because that is the mode, or disposition, of the texts themselves. These texts have to do with the ultimate matter of Truth—which is, therefore, beyond action, beyond all purposiveness.*
>
> *The texts I have selected in this book have no direct concern for social morality, and so forth. Nonetheless, they invariably mention that this is an Ultimate Teaching, only for those who have developed up to a point, and that there are preliminaries required. It is presumed that one who was receiving these Teachings must have brought the body-mind under control, have disciplined it, purified it. As such a practitioner, you are mature enough to receive the Ultimate Teaching, because you are free enough in your energy and attention to examine the Great Matter and realize it to be true. You do not need any argument other than the Truth Itself. All of that has become unnecessary because of your state of preparedness.*

The enterprises of social morality are largely in the domain of the common social order of the first three stages of life, the common world. Conventional religion is largely a political and social institution that exists to bring about an idealization of human behavior, to bring people to function in a manner that is expected socially. It is not about Realization. It is about social morality.

Having sufficiently gone through that school, and the schools beyond that—the esoteric kind of training that purifies and balances and straightens—then there is the Ultimate Teaching. That is the context in which all of these Reality-Teachings have appeared. It is always in a context beyond the active life.

These texts are not a general message to everybody: "Stop all of your activity and just contemplate." This Teaching is only uttered to uniquely prepared individuals.

—FEBRUARY 1, 2006

The preparation for practicing Ultimate Teachings is necessarily a process of calming and bringing to order the otherwise casually wandering energies of body and mind. What was prized traditionally as a sign of true preparation was the virtue of Yogic equanimity, attained by purification and discipline. Shankara is highly praised by Adi Da Samraj as the individual in the Great Tradition who most fully acknowledged and insisted upon the entire range of preliminary practices for anyone who aspires to the non-dual Truth:

Shankara's teachings embrace the totality of the tradition of Hinduism, which was the tradition within which he was active. He covers modes of discipline and approach that correspond to what I call the stages of life. He accounts for devotional practice (Bhakti Yoga), Karma Yoga, Raja Yoga, Kundalini Yoga, and so on, as well as Jnana Yoga as the ultimate mode of practice. He also accounts for sannyas as being the mode of life-discipline associated with Ultimate Realization. He was not teaching in any mode that was dissociated from the Yogic traditions (such as the Kundalini tradition). He simply understood those traditions as preliminary to the ultimate process.

So do I. I have My own language relative to all that. The particularities and details of My own Teaching are unique. But nevertheless, they coincide with Shankara's tradition of understanding.

—APRIL 21, 2005

A relatively recent expression of the traditional wisdom that preliminary practice is necessary is found in an exchange between Swami Vivekananda and a householder devotee, Haripada Mitra:

"Swamiji, will you kindly chalk out the path that I should follow?" Swamiji replied, "First, try to bring the mind under control, no matter what the process is. Everything else will follow as a matter of course. And knowledge—the non-dualistic realization—is very hard to attain. Know that to be the highest human goal. But before one reaches there, one has to make a long preparation and a prolonged effort. The company of holy men and dispassion are the means to it. There is no other way."[4]

DISCRIMINATING BETWEEN DUALISM AND NON-DUALISM

What has been understood traditionally as "non-dual" Realization is not always what Shankara and the Sages represented in this book mean by "non-dual". Shankara's point of view is clear in the following quotation from *Viveka-Chudamani,* one of the principal treatises traditionally attributed to him:

Give up identification with (the physical body and its) family, clan, name, form, and stage of life. These are based on nothing better than a rotting corpse. Give up also the attributes of the

*subtle body, such as the feeling that one does acts and enjoys indi-
vidual experiences. Realize your true nature as undifferentiated
unbroken bliss.*[5]

Shankara is indicating here that true Realization is beyond both the
gross and the subtle dimensions. In his understanding, there is no "one"
left in the Realized state, but only the One Reality. In contrast, other traditions and texts speak of a dualistic Realization—the continuance of a
conscious distinction between the individual self and the Absolute, even
in the experience of union, expressed through such typical phrasings as
"the self and world are, themselves, Divine", indicating that there is some
"one" (or a "self") that is presumed to "survive" in the Realized state.

In His Instruction on how to apply the tool of the seven stages of
life to understanding the traditions, Adi Da Samraj points to just such
differences as this. In Avatar Adi Da's seven stages paradigm, Shankara
represents the sixth stage point of view, while the point of view that "the
self and the world are, themselves, Divine" is describing a Realization of
the fifth stage type. As Avatar Adi Da points out, that fifth stage point
of view is not, in fact, non-dual—even though it may seem to be so, and
is often claimed to be so.

Adi Da Samraj says that the basic sixth stage understanding and
Realization is the pinnacle of the Great Tradition. However, as He has
Revealed, in the seventh stage of life there is a further unfolding of Truth.
The fact that conditions appear to exist ceases to be an issue that must
be resolved—either by declaring conditions to be "Divine" in the fifth
stage manner, or by seeking to turn away from conditions and affirm the
exclusive Reality of Consciousness, in the sixth stage manner.

In the seventh stage of life, there is no need to account for the worlds
of experience. There is no difference between "outer" and "inner" and
"root". The gross, subtle, and causal structure is seen to be just the functional psycho-physical design of the human body-mind, and even of all
of conditional existence. Beyond the entire esoteric anatomy, there is
only Conscious Light, the "Bright", the One Reality and Truth, in and

as which all conditions arise and pass as mere modifications. Thus, in the seventh stage of life, there is, in Adi Da's phrase, the "Divine Self-Recognition" of all that seems to appear.

Another of the traditional arguments to which Adi Da Samraj refers extensively in these pages is the debate between Advaita Vedanta and Buddhism. His insight into the philosophical, historical, and cultural roots of their differences—and into their inherent underlying unity (illuminated in His renderings of their great texts)—is an unparalleled contribution to the understanding of how non-dualism has been interpreted and practiced in the Great Tradition.

THE "RADICAL" UNDERSTANDING OF THE EGO

Going beyond dualism in real practice, rather than as mere philosophy, is a great matter. It means transcending the dual structure of conventional awareness—the sense of self and other, or the "I" over against everything else—in a process that can be called "ego-death". Oriental culture, on the whole, takes a negative view of the body and of physical, or gross, existence. Thus, there is a tendency to dissociate from conditions and to idealize the ascetic life as a way to minimize or eliminate the ego and "get to" What is Beyond. But, as Adi Da Samraj has always pointed out, asceticism—in and of itself—does not lead to true "ego-death", because it is, ultimately, an attempt by the ego to eliminate the ego! To really transcend the ego-"I", which is the most fundamental structure in consciousness, requires a more "radical" (or fundamental) approach.

When Adi Da Samraj began His formal Teaching-Work in 1972, He expounded His own radical understanding of what the ego-"I" is, as opposed to the traditional understanding.

Ramana Maharshi[6] *advised seekers to find out who it is that asks the question, thinks the thought, and so on. But that "who" is, in Reality, not an "entity". When Ramana Maharshi spoke, He used the symbolic language of Advaita Vedanta. . . . The imagery of this traditional description of the process of Realizing Truth deals in statics, "things"-in-space. Therefore, in that traditional description, there is the ego—the objectified, solidified self.*

But I speak in terms of process, or movement. I speak in terms of concepts of experience with which the modern mind is more familiar—and which more accurately reflect the actual nature of conditionally manifested reality. Thus, I do not speak of the ego as an "object" within a conceptual universe of objects. The concept of the "static ego" is no longer very useful—and, indeed, it is false and misleading.

Therefore, what has traditionally been called "the ego" is rightly understood to be an activity. And "radical" self-understanding is that direct seeing of the fundamental (and always present) activity that is suffering, ignorance, distraction, motivation, and dilemma. When that activity is most perfectly understood, then there is Spontaneous and Non-conditional Realization of That Which had previously been excluded from conscious awareness—That Which Is Always Already the Case.[7]

The ego-activity, as Adi Da Samraj has always emphasized, is self-contraction, a recoil in conscious awareness. From this ego-act stem all our notions about reality. We see an apparent world of separate beings and things from a point of awareness that we call "I". This is the world we presume to live in, the world we think is real. But it is real only from a limited point of view. And it is not a "free" world. It is a world fraught with the bondage of frenetic seeking—the never-ending search to overcome the core ego stress that is our fundamental and self-created suffering.

This is the root not only of the searches of ordinary life, but of the religious and spiritual quest as well. As Adi Da Samraj teaches, human beings simply want to fulfill their ego-search, in whatever dimension of reality is their focus—gross, subtle, or causal. The ego-search at the gross level is the wandering in all the possibilities of the waking body-mind. The same search at the subtle level is the pursuit of mystical experience and "spiritual" goals. The causal level of the search is the effort to get beyond all experience and all sense of "I" through one or another technique.

As a young man of only twenty years old, Adi Da Samraj made the "radical" discovery that the very search for Truth is the obstruction to Realizing Truth, because seeking is always based on the presumption and activity of separation from That Which Exists.

I saw that the Truth or Reality was a matter of the absence of all contradictions, of every trace of conflict, opposition, division, or desperate motivation within. Where there is no seeking, no contradiction, there is only the Non-conditional Knowledge and Power that is Reality. This was the first aspect of that sudden Clarity.

In this State beyond all contradiction, I also saw that Freedom and Joy is not attained, that It is not dependent on any form, object, idea, progress, or experience.[8]

Adi Da Samraj sometimes refers to the first six stages of life as the "psycho-biography" of the ego, because these stages represent all the potential that the apparent persona can experience or achieve. In the midst of that vast range of possibility, however, the fundamental ego-activity, the motivated search, remains the same. At the causal depth, all that is left is the root ego, the barest sense of separateness, just the awareness of "I" and "other", and the effort to resolve that last duality. That is the place where the greatest Sages, some of them represented in this book, have "leapt off" the edge into the non-dual Knowledge of the Transcendental Self, or the Nirvanic Truth.

That is the place to which the youthful Adi Da Samraj constantly returned in His intensive investigation of the question: "What *is* consciousness?" He knew intuitively that the Truth lay in understanding the mysterious coincidence between the Transcendental Reality and the apparent world. The answer that ultimately came—through the force of His own "radical" self-understanding—enabled Him to transcend all the partial messages of Truth delivered through the psycho-physics of the body-mind and to Re-Awaken to the "Bright", the Inherently egoless Condition, beyond all seeking and all "difference".

It is Adi Da's Abiding as the "Bright" that provides the foundation for the renderings given in this book and for His commentaries upon them—and also for the Reality-Way of Adidam altogether. At the same time, Adidam does not, as He says here, appear "in a vacuum":

> *There is an authoritative source-tradition within the Great Tradition, with which the Reality-Way of Adidam is continuous, and which, therefore, provides a basis for understanding the Reality-Way of Adidam. The uniqueness of the Reality-Way I have Revealed and Given does not exist in a vacuum. The Reality-Way of Adidam is, ultimately, the Perfect Tradition, but there is a dimension at the heights of all the Transcendentalist (or sixth stage) schools within the Great Tradition that is compatible with It—simply lacking the final step, which is the seventh stage of life.*
>
> *Thus, the Reality-Way of Adidam exists with reference to the Great Tradition, but it is a universal Teaching, not an Eastern teaching.*
>
> —APRIL 21, 2005, AND MARCH 3, 2006

The special relationship of the Reality-Way of Adidam to Advaita Vedanta and Buddhism is made clear in this book. There is much in Avatar Adi Da's renderings of these principal traditional texts that could come directly out of His own Teaching. These traditional texts point to a true comprehension and Realization of Reality As It Is. Some statements and passages are clearly resonant with the seventh stage of life, in which there is no "difference" between Consciousness Itself and the arising world. Taken as a whole, however, these texts do not show the signs of a *complete* understanding and Realization.

Nevertheless, in order to plainly indicate that the Reality-Way of Adidam is continuous with the traditions of Advaita Vedanta and

Buddhism—and the actual *completion* of these traditions (and the entire Great Tradition)—Adi Da Samraj has given alternative names to Adidam that indicate this connection and continuity, including "Advaitayana Buddhism", and "Buddhayana Advaitism".[9]

Adidam both combines and transcends the two different orientations represented by Buddhism and Advaita Vedanta—the emphasis (in Buddhism) on discriminating what is merely conditional, or "not-self", and the emphasis (in Advaita Vedanta) on directly identifying with the Absolute Reality, or Transcendental Self. Adi Da Samraj points to the possibility of transcending the ego on the basis of a "dual sensitivity"—a sensitivity to what is merely conditional and passing, on the one hand, and to what is Non-conditional, Transcendental, and Divine, on the other.

The means of this dual sensitivity is not "mindfulness" (in the Buddhist sense) or a discriminative effort to locate the Ultimate Reality beyond objects (in the Advaitic sense). The means of practice and of Realization in the Reality-Way of Adidam is Adi Da Samraj Himself and His direct Transmission of the "Bright", the Conscious Light That Is Reality.

Those who are Graced to sit at the Feet of a Master enter into the sphere of the Master's Radiance, the "field" of his or her innate Transmission of the state of Realization. The Words of Adi Da Samraj carry a potency that is far beyond the verbal meaning, a force that activates fundamental transformations. This potency is not restricted to hearing Him speak. He also invests Himself Spiritually in all of His Writing, and that Transmission of His Person can be received through reading any of His books, such as the one before you now.

I

To Realize Nirvana Is To Realize The True Self

Buddhist Realism and Its (Ultimately) Inherent Sympathy With Advaitic Idealism

An Essay by Avatar Adi Da Samraj

Traditional Buddhism (in all its forms, and especially in its original, or classical, formulation) is based upon an analysis of conditional existence. And that analysis is associated with two key propositions. The first of these two key propositions is that the fundamental characteristic of conditional existence (or conditional being) is (inherently, and necessarily) that of <u>suffering</u>. And the second of these two key propositions is that suffering (and, therefore, conditional existence, or conditional being, itself) can be made to cease (or to become <u>un</u>-"caused").

The Buddhist proposition that conditional existence <u>is</u> (itself, or inherently) suffering is not based merely on the practical observation that life can be difficult, and pain can be suffered, and eventual death is inevitable for all. Rather, the Buddhist equation of conditional existence and suffering is based on the summary insight (founded on constant observation) that conditional existence (or every moment and kind of conditional being or event) is only <u>conditionally</u> existing (or existing due to some, necessarily transitory, "cause"). Therefore, according to the Buddhist analysis, conditional existence is (in addition to being

16

always, and inherently, characterized by suffering) also (and always, and inherently) characterized by change (or impermanence) and by the lack of "self" (or of substantively real, rather than merely apparently real, independence and separateness, or separability). That is to say, because conditional existence is always only conditionally existing (or existing only as a "caused effect"), no form or state of conditional existence is permanent (or eternally existing), and no conditionally existing thing or conditionally existing being substantively exists independently, or separately, or separably, or <u>absolutely</u> (as if it were not a "caused" and temporary and utterly dependently arising "effect").

The purpose (or intended result) of this "realistic" Buddhist analysis of conditional existence is not despair but disenchantment (or <u>release</u> from un-"realistic" illusions about conditional existence). And, for those who are deeply convinced of the fundamental factuality (or undeniability) of this analysis, the Buddhist philosophical systems offer a "solution" to the "problem" of conditional existence. That "solution" (in each and all of its traditional forms) is the "Dharma" (Law, Teaching, Way, or Process) of <u>un</u>-"causing" (or ceasing to "cause") conditional existence (or conditional being) itself.

The Ultimate Message of traditional Buddhist Dharma is not merely that conditional existence is conditional (or "caused", and, therefore, incapable of either permanency or Ultimate Fulfillment), but that conditional existence is not necessary. That is to say, traditional Buddhist Dharma affirms that whatever is "caused" can be un-"caused" (or cease to be "caused"). Thus, the Buddhist Way is (fundamentally, and always) about understanding and (via understanding, and its various associated means) releasing the fundamental "cause" of conditional existence. And, according to the traditional Buddhist analysis, the fundamental "cause" of conditional existence—or, more precisely, the fundamental "cause" of conditional being, as a human (or otherwise dependently arising and conditionally, or phenomenally, "self"-aware) "entity"—is <u>desire</u> (or craving, or clinging).

Thus, fundamentally, traditional Buddhist Dharma is (in any of its forms) a philosophically proposed "method" for the elimination (or the un-"causing") of desire. And the result sought by this "method" is both the peace of desirelessness (or inherent freedom from either clinging or avoidance relative to the positives and negatives of life) and the Awakening to the Ultimate (or Nirvanic) Condition—Which Condition is Prior to all "causes" and all "effects", and Which Condition is (therefore) inherently without connection to (or limitation by) conditional existence (and the categories, characteristics, and "experiences" of conditional existence).

The Realization of the Nirvanic Condition is the Ultimate Goal of traditional Buddhism (in all its forms). In fact, positively descriptive references to the Nirvanic Condition do appear even in the earliest Buddhist texts[1]—wherein, for example, the Nirvanic Condition is described as "the Unborn, the Unoriginated, the Unmade, the Uncompounded", "infinite consciousness" and "final bliss", and "Consciousness, without distinguishing mark, infinite and shining everywhere—here the material elements do not penetrate . . . but here it is that the conditioned consciousness ceases to be".[2] However, especially the classical (or "Hinayana") form of Buddhism is, in general, rather characteristically associated with a refusal to positively describe (or to propose direct descriptions of) the Nirvanic Condition—because (according to the "point of view" of classical Buddhist "realism") any direct conceptual description of the Nirvanic Condition would necessarily be based on the inherently limited (and limiting) categories of conditional mind, and would (therefore) tend to be misleading, or (at least) not fruitful relative to the actual attainment of the Nirvanic Condition. Therefore, especially the classical formulations of Buddhism rather rigorously confine themselves to a "realistic" analysis of conditional existence—as a "caused" (or dependently arising) process, characterized by suffering (or the inherent lack of capability for Ultimate Fulfillment), and by change (or the inherent lack of capability for permanence), and by utter dependency (or "emptiness", which is the inherent lack of capability for substantive "selfness", or independence, or separation from the stream of "causes" and "effects"). And, on the basis of right application to that analysis (which the, especially classical, Buddhist schools recommend be made the subject of a profoundly meditative, or "mindful", observation of "experience"), it is traditionally presumed that the inherently indescribable Nirvanic Condition will, in due course (and without recourse to any "idealistic", or positively descriptive, propositions), be Realized.

However, because of their characteristic reluctance to positively (or directly) describe the Nirvanic Condition (Itself), the proponents of traditional (especially classical) Buddhism tend to exhibit a rather dogmatic (and apparently non-comprehending) attitude when confronted by the more "idealistic" (or positively descriptive) philosophical propositions of other traditions (and of the more "idealistic" schools within the general tradition of Buddhism itself). And the principal doctrine that is the usual justification for the non-comprehending resistance of (especially classical) Buddhism to other (generally "idealistic", or positively descriptive) propositions about the Nature of the Nirvanic Condition (or the Ultimate, or non-"caused", Reality) is the doctrine of "anatta" (or of the "no-self" characteristic).

The Buddhist doctrine of "anatta" (or of the "no-self" characteristic) is, simply, an extension of the basic Buddhist perception that what arises conditionally cannot be made either perfect or permanent, but that it can, by a right (and tacit) understanding, be transcended. Thus, the Buddhist doctrine of "anatta" thoroughly insists that whatever is conditionally arising and changing and passing away cannot be "self"— because whatever is "self" must, by definition, be inherent (rather than "caused") and unchanging (or of fixed characteristics), and all that is "self" must be within the "self's" own power of determination. Likewise, the Buddhist doctrine of "anatta" (which is inseparably connected to the Buddhist doctrines of "suffering" and of "impermanence") is rooted in a characteristic feeling-presumption, that it is both ignorant and futile (and entirely an unnecessary bother) to make efforts to perpetuate what is not "self" (or, in other words, to cling to whatever is conditional, impermanent, and incapable of Ultimate Fulfillment), but that it is always both intelligent and auspicious (and conducive toward the Realization of Inherent Nirvanic Freedom) to discipline and relinquish the motive and effort to perpetuate (or even to indulge in) whatever is not "self".

The doctrine of "anatta" is, simply, that portion of the original Buddhist analysis of conditional existence that is associated with the observation that no conditionally existing being is self-originated (or non-"caused", eternal, and substantively separable, separate, and independent), but all conditionally existing beings are (as conditionally existing beings) dependently arising (or "caused"), and they are thoroughly dependent (for their conditional existence) on the totality of even all "causes". In fact, that proposition (of "anatta") is only one particular (and inseparable) portion of a larger argument—which is that conditional existence is always and only conditional (or "caused", and limited, and changing, and dependent). And the purpose of that larger argument is to provide a foundation (of disenchantment) upon which the ultimate Buddhist argument may be found to be convincing. And that ultimate Buddhist argument is that "caused" existence can cease to be "caused", such that Nirvanic ("Unborn", or Most Prior, and not at all "caused") Existence may be Realized.

Therefore, the doctrine of "anatta" is simply (or specifically, and only) a "realistic" proposition about phenomenal (or conditional) being. The doctrine of "anatta" is not (itself) an "idealistic" (or even metaphysical) proposition. Rather, the doctrine of "anatta" is an inseparable part of a consistently "realistic" argument that, characteristically, refuses to make "idealistic" (or even metaphysical) propositions. Therefore, the doctrine of "anatta" is not an inherently metaphysical (or negatively "idealistic") statement such as: "There is no Absolute Atman (or Ultimate Absolute Nature of Being)." Rather, the doctrine of "anatta" is, simply (or specifically, and only), intended to be a "realistic" argument for the relinquishment of desire for conditional existence. And, because that relinquishment is proposed (in the classical Buddhist formulation) to be the very means whereby the Nirvanic Condition may be Realized, it can (rightly) be said that the doctrine of "anatta" is a "realistic" Buddhist means for proposing (or pointing toward, but not conceptually <u>defining</u>) the Nirvanic Condition (or the Ultimate Absolute Reality Itself).

Many proponents of the classical formulations of Buddhism argue that the doctrine of "anatta" is a specific denial of the Truth, or Reality, of the Brahmanic Atman (or the Ultimate and Non-Dual and Inherently Non-"caused" Reality, as described in the schools of traditional Indian Advaitism, and suggested, using different technical terms, in many of the "Mahayana" schools, including the "Vajrayana" schools, of traditional Buddhism). However, the dogmatic refusal to (at least tacitly) affirm or comprehend the Brahmanic Atman (and other positively descriptive, or "idealistic", propositions of the Ultimate Absolute Condition) is immediately transcended as soon as there is a fully correct understanding of both the "anatta" doctrine and the "Brahmanic Atman" doctrine (and the likenesses to the doctrine of the Brahmanic Atman, which are to be found even in the more "idealistic" schools of the Buddhist tradition itself).

The Advaitic doctrine of the true (Brahmanic, or Ultimate) Atman is a description of the Ultimate Absolute Condition That Is Identical to Brahman (the Non-"caused", or Self-Existing, and Ultimate, and Infinitely Self-Radiant Reality That Is the Perfectly Subjective Source-Condition of conditional existence). That Ultimate (or Brahmanic) Atman (Which Is the Most Prior, and Realizable, Self-Condition of every apparent, or conditionally existing, being) is not a part of the conditional "self", but It Is the Absolute and Non-conditional State (or true Self-Condition), in Which the conditionally manifested being (or dependently arising psycho-physical "entity") is (apparently) arising. Indeed, the Brahmanic Atman corresponds (in Reality, and by definition) to the Buddhist definition of true "self" (properly, spelled with a capital "S"). Therefore, the proposed Atman That <u>Is</u> Brahman Is, by means of an "idealistic" (or positively descriptive) conception, the Very and Same Reality That is (even via such "realistic" Buddhist conceptions as the "anatta" doctrine) referred (or pointed) to as the Nirvanic Condition.

The Brahmanic Atman is inherently empty of conditionality, separateness, change, limitation, suffering, and desire. Therefore, it is not possible to "cling to" the Brahmanic Atman (Itself). The Brahmanic Atman can be Realized only by transcending the conditional "self" (and all clinging to conditional existence). Therefore, the Brahmanic Atman can be Realized only As the Nirvanic Absolute (Inherently Most Prior to conditional existence). For this reason, there is an inherent Sympathy (and a necessary equation to be made) between the Buddhist proposition of the Nirvanic Condition and the Advaitic proposition of the Brahmanic Atman. This Sympathy (and this equation) is obvious to all actual Realizers (whatever their tradition may be) of That Which Inherently Transcends conditional existence. And all others (not yet Thus Realized) are best served if they (most tolerantly) regard the doctrine of "anatta" (which appeals to the "realistic" logic of "causation") and the doctrine of the "Brahmanic Atman" (which appeals to the logic of Prior Being) as two distinct but (fundamentally) compatible (and even complementary) arguments (one "realistic" and the other "idealistic") for the Realization of the Non-conditional Reality That Is Obvious When the conditional reality is transcended.

II

THERE IS A NON-CONDITIONAL CONDITION TO BE REALIZED

The Reality-Teachings of The Buddhist Sage Gotama Sakyamuni

An epitome of the Teachings of Gotama Sakyamuni,
the original Master-Sage of traditional Buddhism—
rendered from key statements found in the earliest canon
of Buddhist scriptures

The collection of texts rendered by Adi Da Samraj in "There Is A Non-conditional Condition To Be Realized" has been drawn (by Him) from the Pali Canon, the primary collection of early Buddhist scriptures. The Pali Canon (so called because it is recorded in the Pali language) is grouped into three sections, or "baskets" (pitaka), relating to (1) the rules of monastic discipline (Vinaya-pitaka), (2) the discourses of Gotama Sakyamuni (Sutta-pitaka), and (3) further teachings (Abhidhamma-pitaka). Adi Da Samraj has rendered selected verses of various texts found in the second "basket", containing the discourses and dialogues ascribed to Gotama Sakyamuni (ca. fifth century BCE). The texts of the Pali Canon were first preserved and transmitted orally by Buddhist monks and were later codified on palm-leaf manuscripts, likely around the time of the common era or somewhat before.

The Sage Gotama Sakyamuni, traditionally referred to by the honorific title "Buddha" (signifying one who is a Master-Sage "of Self-Illuminated Mind"), said to His disciples:

1. Whatever and all that arises (or originates) conditionally, or as the effect of a cause, will (inevitably, and necessarily) cease—or come to an end, and pass away.

   MAJJHIMA NIKAYA 56

2. Conditionally arising forms and experiences are, necessarily, impermanent and fleeting. Therefore, they cannot satisfy (or even console) the person desiring to be fulfilled, or who is seeking a lasting happiness. True satisfaction (or true happiness) is only in the transcending of all desires—and of all seeking—for conditionally arising (or causable) forms and experiences. Indeed, real liberation from desire is the only true and final satisfaction— and the final transcending of all seeking is the only true and real liberation.

   ANGUTTARA NIKAYA VII, 62

3. Perfect peace is the only perfect satisfaction, or real happiness. Perfect peace is in the perfect transcending of desire—or of all seeking toward satisfaction (or fulfillment, or happiness) by means of conditionally arising, and necessarily impermanent, forms and experiences. Perfect peace is Realized in the non-arising—and, indeed, in the non-causing—of impermanent conditions, forms, and experiences. In the non-arising—and, therefore, the non-desiring, and, altogether, the non-seeking—of impermanent conditions, forms, and experiences, there is perfect peace. The perfect peace Realized in the transcending of all conditionality is true liberation—or Nirvana.

   ANGUTTARA NIKAYA III, 32

4. My teaching argument is entirely and only in the indication that conditional existence is suffering—because it is inherently impermanent,
and, therefore, unable to grant true and permanent satisfaction. My
teaching admonition is entirely and only in the indication that all suffering can be transcended (or escaped), by means of the transcending
of all efforts of desire and seeking toward impermanent conditions,
forms, and experiences—and, indeed, by means of the transcending
of all attachment to conditional (or impermanent) existence itself.

Majjhima Nikaya 22

5. Suffering arises (inherently, and necessarily) whenever any conditional (or caused, and, therefore, impermanent) form, experience, or
state arises—or even whenever any causative effort (of desire, or of
seeking) arises toward conditional possibilities (of form, experience,
or state). Therefore, suffering ceases (or is inherently transcended)
only whenever causative efforts (of desire, and of seeking) cease
(or are inherently transcended), and (thus and thereby) conditionally causable forms, experiences, and states are no longer arising (or
causing suffering).

Samyutta Nikaya XII, 15

6. No person of right understanding attributes separate (or self-
existing, and non-dependent, and non-conditional) existence to
any conditionally arising (or conditionally caused, and inherently
impermanent) form, experience, or state. Therefore, no person of
right understanding should regard (or interpret) any conditionally arising (or conditionally caused, and inherently impermanent)
form, experience, or state to be a separate (or self-existing, and non-
dependent, and non-conditional) "self"—or a real and permanent
(or even eternal) ego-"I".

Majjhima Nikaya 115

7. All persons who conceive (and advocate the existence) of a real and permanent (and even eternal) ego-"I" (or separate "self", or eternal "soul") are attributing "selfhood" to what is "objectively" apparent (and, therefore, "not-self")—and, as such, they are attributing permanence (as well as separateness, and even self-existence) to what is merely conditionally, and temporarily, and dependently caused. Therefore, such persons (in their ignorant worldliness) conceive of material "objectivity", and emotional feelings, and perceptual states, and states of mind, and, indeed, every kind of attention-awareness to be a real, and permanent, and even eternal, and separate, and non-dependent, and even self-existing entity (or "self", or ego-"I").

Samyutta Nikaya XXII, 47

8. Whatever is an "object" of attention—or, that is to say, whatever stands in apparent "objective" relation to attention-awareness—is not "self". Attention (or attention-awareness) itself is not "self"— and not a "self". All causes of attention-awareness are not "self". All forms, conditions, or states of attention-awareness are not "self" (and not a "self"). Therefore, how could it be possible that "consciousness"—defined or limited by the idea that it arises from (or is caused by, or, in any sense, depends upon) whatever is not "self"—is "self" (or a "self", or the "self")? Conditionally arising "consciousness" is merely attention-awareness—impermanent, conditionally caused, only suffering, never satisfied, always desiring, always seeking, not liberated, not at peace, not Nirvana.

Samyutta Nikaya XXXV, 141

9. All of the process of conditional causation and all of the phenomena that are conditionally caused must be observed, and understood, and transcended as such. The presumption (or idea) of a separate "self" (or ego-"I") is conditionally caused, and based upon the perception of conditionally arising phenomena—all of

which are not "self". Therefore, the presumption (or idea) of a separate "self" (or ego-"I")—including all of its impulses of desire and seeking—must be observed, and understood, and transcended as "<u>not-self</u>".

ANGUTTARA NIKAYA VI, 104

10. In the deep solitude
    inherent in the heart,
    the happiness
    transcending human conditions
    is "located"—
    by one who knows
    the perfect Realization
    of Truth.

    Observing the arising
    and passing
    of conditionally caused
    forms, experiences, and states—
    the Realizer of
    the perfect knowing
    of Truth
    transcends the ego-"I"
    in Transcendental Bliss,
    while Self-Beholding
    the inherently egoless Condition
    of the birthless and deathless State.

DHAMMAPADA 373f

11. All conditionally arising
    forms, experiences, and states
    are impermanent and brief.
    The only law

of all causes and of all effects

is,

at first,

to make a sudden appearance,

and,

second,

to make an equally sudden disappearance.

Having come in an instant,

they, likewise, are gone.

Indifference to this

always observable cycle

is happiness.

Perfect freedom from this

always observable cycle

is liberation.

Digha Nikaya 16

12. Attention-awareness becomes the idea of an ego-"I" (or a separate "self") by means of an apparent duality—or the experienced division between the function (or organ) of perception and the "objects" of perception. The function (or organ) of perception is only conditionally arising, conditionally caused, dependent, impermanent, always changing, and always recoiling on itself (as if it were a separate ego-"I"). Likewise, the apparent "objects" of perception are (all) only conditionally arising, conditionally caused, dependent, impermanent, always changing, and always recoiling on themselves (or seeming to become other, "objective", separate, and only as they seem). Because attention-awareness and its apparent "objects" are always mutually and merely conditionally (and impermanently) arising (by means of mutual causation), right understanding merely (or indifferently) observes what is conditionally arising and impermanent—and, thus and thereby, transcends both the idea of an ego-"I" (or a separate, non-conditional, non-dependent, and per-

manent "self") and (thus and thereby) all attachment to the conditionally apparent "objects" of attention.

SAMYUTTA NIKAYA XXXV, 93, 155

13. The mere (or indifferent) observing of all that is conditionally arising and impermanent should be cultivated (or intensively practiced), in order that the idea of an ego-"I" (or separate "self") may be entirely eliminated (or perfectly transcended). The Realization that ego-"I" is really __not__ "self" becomes established in one who intensively (and indifferently) observes all that is merely conditionally arising and impermanent. Therefore, the idea of an ego-"I" (or separate "self") is (in due course) perfectly transcended in one who practices mere (or indifferent) observing of all that is conditionally arising and impermanent—and the Realization of the perfect transcending of all that is __not__ "self" __is__ Nirvana.

UDANA IV, 1

14. In Truth, there __is__ a non-conditional Condition—wherein there are no material or otherwise "objective" forms, conditions, experiences, or states. That Condition is neither in nor of this world— nor is It in or of any other conditionally arising world. I call this Truth-Condition __That__ which neither arises nor passes away. It neither changes nor remains always the same (as an unchanging conditional appearance). It is not conditionally caused, conditionally apparent, conditionally developing, or conditionally sustained. It is neither born nor subject to death (or cessation). It is That wherein (or __as__ Which) __all__ suffering is transcended and ended and not existing.

UDANA VIII, 1

15. There __is__ a non-conditional Condition. That non-conditional Condition is not caused, not conditionally originated, not born, not "created", not separately rendered as any kind of conditionally

appearing form. If there were <u>no</u> such non-conditional Condition, escape from this world—or the transcending of even <u>all</u> that is merely caused, conditionally originated, born, seemingly "created", or separately rendered as the kinds of conditionally appearing form—<u>would</u> <u>not</u> <u>be</u> <u>possible</u>. However, escape from this world—and, indeed, the transcending of even <u>all</u> that is of a merely conditionally apparent nature—<u>is</u> <u>perfectly</u> <u>possible</u>. Escape—or the real transcending of <u>all</u> conditionality—is perfectly possible <u>only</u> because there <u>is</u> a non-conditional (and acausal) Condition.

UDANA VIII, 3

III

THE TRANSCENDENTAL TRUTH
OF REALITY

The Reality-Teachings of The Buddhist Sage Nagarjuna

From the Mahayanavimsaka,
traditionally attributed to the principal
"Mahayana" Buddhist Master-Sage, Nagarjuna

The Mahayanavimsika, *or "Twenty Verses on the Great Vehicle", is traditionally ascribed to the Buddhist philosopher Nagarjuna, who lived in South India in the second to third century CE. There is insufficient evidence to definitively establish the historicity of this ascription. Nagarjuna founded the Madhyamaka school of Buddhism, a philosophical movement which emphasized the doctrine of the Middle Way,* madhyamaka, *and the teaching of emptiness,* sunyata-vada. *Originally composed in Sanskrit, the text survives in multiple variants in Sanskrit, Chinese, and Tibetan, which differ in the number and content of the verses.*

1. The Transcendentally Enlightened Master at the origin of the tradition of Buddhist teachings is honored by the title "Buddha"—signifying one who is of Self-Illuminated mind. A Buddha is a

31

perfect renunciate, transcending all attachment to conditional existence. The state of a Buddha is limitless and perfectly capable to Self-Illuminate the minds of all beings. By virtue of inherently compassionate heart-fullness, a Buddha Self-Reveals the otherwise unspeakable Transcendental (or non-conditional, and acausal) Truth to all beings.

2. In the Transcendental state (or non-conditional Condition) that is Truth itself, there is no conditionality—no conditional causation, no arising of conditional effects of conditional causation, and no cessation (or coming to an end) of any conditional effects of conditional causation. A true Buddha, or Transcendentally Self-Illuminated Master, is, by virtue of the Self-Illuminated Transcendental state that characterizes the Transcendental Truth itself, not other than the Transcendental state that is Truth itself. Therefore, a true Buddha is only the Transcendental Truth itself—inherently without conditionality, and (therefore) inherently free of the conditional characteristic of either being (or having been) caused to exist or (otherwise) being (or having been) caused to not exist. Even all beings are of the same essential nature as any true Buddha—because every true Buddha is identical to the Transcendental Truth of all.

3. The non-conditional Condition of all is not the cause of this or any other conditionally apparent world. Every conditionally apparent entity, or form, or world of entities and forms originates only and entirely from (or as a caused result of) other (or previous) conditions. Only conditional causes originate conditional effects. There is no perfectly prior causative nature (or "Creator-God") underlying whatever is conditionally appearing. What is underlying and perfectly prior is the Transcendental Truth, the Buddha-nature, the perfectly acausal (or inherently actionless and non-conditional) Condition of all conditions (or of all conditional and mutually dependent causes and effects). Therefore, the non-conditional

Condition of all conditions is, in and of itself, formless and empty (or void of conditional and causative characteristics). This understanding (or non-conditional knowledge) of the Transcendental Truth of Reality is the unique Transcendental knowledge that is Self-Evident to a true Transcendentally Self-Illuminated Master (whose knowledge is inherently perfect).

4. The Transcendental (or non-conditional and acausal, or inherently actionless) Condition of all conditionally appearing entities, forms, and worlds is (as such) like a mirror, in which all conditionally caused appearances are like mere reflections. When mere reflections are seen from the perspective of the mirror in which they are (indifferently) reflected—they are found (or understood) to be of the same nature as the mirror itself. Therefore, right understanding knows all conditionally apparent (or conditionally caused) entities, forms, and worlds non-conditionally (or acausally)—and, thus, as essentially formless, empty (of the implications of apparent conditional characteristics), non-dual (or free of the effects of the apparent dynamics of mutually opposite qualities or motions), and always already as is (or inherently without change or impermanence).

5. Those who are without right understanding, and yet bound to the implications of conditionally apparent causes and effects (appearing, to their view, as impermanent and limited entities, forms, worlds, experiences, and states), attribute separate, independent existence—and even existence as a separate "self"—to what is not separate, not independent, and not "self", but which is only a mutually dependent and indivisible and merely apparent reflection in the Transcendental (or acausal) Condition of all mutually caused conditions. Indeed, those who are without right understanding (and who are, thus, not only apparently in but, also, effectively of the world) are likewise bound to all kinds of equally wrong (or deluded and ego-bound) views—wherein and whereby happiness is sought

where it is not to be found, and misery is found wherein it is not (in Truth) existing, and detachment is presumed when it is not truly achieved, and "self"-discipline is engaged merely as a method of desiring, and liberation is thought to be a causable condition of body and mind.

6. In the Transcendental Condition that is Reality and Truth, no kind of born-existence is caused or experienced, no ascent to high or highest planes of conditional happiness is sought or attained, and no descent to low or lowest planes of conditional suffering is either avoided or endured. This is the case entirely and only because (or as an inherent characteristic) of the inherent nature (or non-conditional and acausal state) of the Transcendental Condition that is Reality and Truth.

7. In the Transcendental Condition that is Reality and Truth, there is no presumption or idea that actions will—in accordance with their characteristic quality or intent—cause change, either in the form of suffered results (such as disease, old age, and death) or in the form of positively desired results (such as health, longevity, immortality, or even happiness, or liberation, itself). This is the case, entirely and only because ideas, and active seeking, and even action itself are not characteristics of the inherent nature (or non-conditional and acausal state) of the Transcendental Condition that is Reality and Truth.

8. It is only because of their lack of right understanding (or tacit Realization) of the inherent nature (or non-conditional and acausal state) of the Transcendental Condition of Reality and Truth that conditionally-born beings are deluded by the appearance of conditionally arising entities, forms, worlds, experiences, and states. As a (thus) caused result of their lack of right understanding, conditionally-born beings embrace wrong (or merely conditionally-

based) views—or ideas, intentions, desires, and goals of causative seeking. Only on that (conditional) basis do apparently born beings seek (and only temporarily achieve) positive and negative planes and states of conditionally caused experience. Thus, conditionally-born beings variously (and always only temporarily) experience conditionally causable results (or conditions)—entirely and only in accordance with the illusions they presume and embrace and activate. The world of conditional possibilities (both high and low) is itself entirely an illusion—or a mere reflection in the Transcendental Condition that *is* Reality and Truth. Therefore, the world of conditional possibilities (both high and low) exists only apparently (and not necessarily)—and entirely as a merely apparent result (or effect) of the causes (or conditions) that are presumed (or otherwise not transcended by virtue of tacit right understanding).

9. As an artist might become terrified by a "self"-deluded encounter with a material creation (or self-fabricated illusion) of his or her own mind and making—so, also, the inherently foolish (or "self"-deluded) ego-"I" (or "self"-presumed separate "self"-entity) is constantly anxious and afraid in the world of conditionally arising entities, forms, experiences, and states. That is to say, the anxiety and fear inherent in the experience of egoity (or of "self"-separateness) are (entirely and only) conditionally caused—and thus caused as a result of a false understanding (or a lack of right understanding) of the conditionally arising world and of the inherent nature (or non-conditional and acausal state) of the Transcendental Condition of Reality and Truth. Therefore, fear (itself) and all worldly anxiety are merely the "self"-caused results of false "knowledge" (or wrong understanding)—and, as this insight suggests, fear (itself) and all worldly anxiety can be transcended, by means of right knowledge, or right understanding, and tacit Realization of the inherent nature of the Transcendental Condition of Reality and Truth.

10. As a careless person may casually and inadvertently lose his or her life by stepping into a deadly trap, such as a swamp of sucking mud, or a torrentially flooded mountain stream—so, also, all ego-bound beings inevitably waste (and, eventually, lose) their lives in the problem-based mind and the countlessly "self"-caused dilemmas of their life-entrapment. Indeed, the ego-"I" cannot escape the trap of mortal bondage—unless the illusion of egoity (or of "self"-separateness) itself is transcended, by means of right knowledge, or right understanding, and tacit Realization of the inherent nature of the Transcendental Condition of Reality and Truth.

11. The discomfortable feelings associated with the dilemmas of "self"-delusion are the results of casually and irrationally presuming merely imagined "things" to exist in "objective" fact. All "self"-caused bondage (or "self"-presumed entrapment) is the direct result of false "knowledge"—wherein and whereby separate, independent, and "objective" existence is attributed to conditionally arising forms, entities, experiences, and states (all of which are only and entirely of the nature of the Transcendental, or non-conditional, Reality and Truth). Therefore, ego-bound (or "self"-presumedly separate) entities (or conditionally apparent beings) always discomfort (and even torment, and, eventually, destroy) themselves—by means of a false understanding of apparent (or merely conditionally arising) forms, entities, experiences, and states of all possible kinds. Only right knowledge—or right understanding of conditionally apparent forms, entities, experiences, and states and (coincidently) tacit Realization of the inherent nature of the Transcendental Condition of Reality and Truth—is (or tacitly Realizes) the inherent transcending of all illusions of "objective" (or of separate and independent) existence.

12. As right understanding works to cure the heart of false "knowledge" and "self"-delusion—more and more, one looks upon the otherwise helpless world through the purified eyes of right knowledge. That

glance of heart-comprehension is (inevitably) touched with over-whelming sympathies, that motivate and grow right life. Therefore, if you grow to view the world of conditionally-born beings from the position of a rightened heart, the heart's inherent compassion will, itself, require and oblige you to exercise all your life in the magnification of right understanding of conditional existence—as an illusory (or non-separate) appearance within the non-conditional (or Transcendental) Condition of all. Thus, and merely by means of your own exercise of right life, based on right understanding (or right knowledge), you also serve the heart-cure of even all conditionally-born beings.

13. When one's own mind and life have become right, purified, and balanced, by means of the inherently compassionate heart-exercise of right understanding, then the necessary fundamental prerequisites for the potential life of a true Buddha have been established. When one is, thereafter, in due course, set perfectly free from <u>all</u> bondage and <u>all</u> false "knowledge"—such that <u>only</u> right knowledge (or fullest right understanding of conditional existence, and tacit perfect Realization of the inherent nature of the Transcendental Condition of Reality and Truth) characterizes the heart, the mind, and the life—then one has become perfectly capable, a true Buddha, a perfect friend of all who otherwise suffer the countlessly enumerated consequences of egoic "self"-causation and egoically "self"-caused bondage.

14. A true Buddha tacitly Realizes the Transcendental Truth by means of the exercise of right understanding of the universally evident cause-and-effect cycle—or the vast mutually dependent pattern of conditionally arising existence, wherein living beings appear, and struggle, and die, always in exact accordance with their states of mind, or "self"-presumed "knowledge", and their thus-determined actions within the vast impermanence of even <u>all</u> conditionally caused conditions. Because a true Buddha attains tacit Realization

of the Transcendental Truth by means of the exercise of right under-standing of the universally evident (and mutually dependent) cycle of cause-and-effect, a true Buddha is characterized by right under-standing of the conditionally arising world of entities, forms, expe-riences, and states—and, thus, by the (inherently right) knowledge that all apparent conditions are inherently without separateness and independence, and that no apparent condition is discretely defin-able (or really self-limited) by any separately self-existing begin-ning, middle, or end, and that, indeed, because there is neither separateness nor independence anywhere, or in and of anything, all of conditional existence (whether of the world or of the presumed ego-"I") is characterized by non-separateness and mutual interde-pendence, inherently void (or empty) of real entification (or sepa-rate and quantifiable "selfness").

15. The arising of caused conditions is merely conditionally apparent. Just so, even the cessation of caused conditions (due to counter-causation, or non-causation)—and, also, the evident non-arising of caused conditions—is merely conditionally apparent. Whether caused conditions arise or not—the experience (or the knowing) of the evidence, in either case, is itself a merely conditionally caused (or conditionally evident) phenomenon or state. Therefore, neither conditional existence nor any kind of process whereby conditional existence is avoided or, by any means, made to cease is the Way of Truth. Truth (itself) is of an inherently Transcendental nature—inherently (or always already) formless, non-conditional, actionless, not caused, and Self-Illuminated (or perfectly Self-Enlightened, acausally, by virtue of its own intrinsic, true, and very Self-nature).

16. The evidently perceived "objects" experienced (or known) in the conditional state of dreaming are no longer perceived when the conditional state of ordinary waking becomes the basis for the pre-sumption of knowledge. That is to say, from the "point of view"

of the waking state, the "objects" (or the states of conditional knowledge) otherwise perceived or presumed in the state of dreaming <u>do</u> <u>not</u> <u>exist</u>. Similarly, in the case of one in whom even the waking-state-ignorance (or wrong understanding) of the world of conditionally arising appearances is transcended—by means of the Self-Illumination inherent in the Transcendental (or non-conditional) Condition of Reality and Truth—even the totality of conditional existence (and all of waking, dreaming, and sleeping "objects" or states) <u>does</u> <u>not</u> <u>exist</u>. In the Self-Illuminated Condition of Transcendental (or non-conditional) Reality and Truth, there is—inherently, or intrinsically—no conditional causation, no conditional arising, and, therefore, no conditional existence.

17. Whatever may be the immediate or otherwise ultimate cause of an illusion—the illusion is nevertheless a mere illusion. When <u>everything</u> is an illusion—or a mere and complex result of conditionally evident causes—then <u>no</u> "thing" (or "object", or "form", or "entity", or "state", or "world") is existing as such. That is to say, conditionally caused "things" (or "beings", or "worlds") do not exist (as separate "things", or "beings", or "worlds")—but <u>only</u> the Transcendental (or non-conditional, and acausal, and non-dual, and non-separate) Reality and Truth is the case, even if conditionally caused "things" (or "beings", or "worlds") appear (or seem) to arise. Only the non-conditional Transcendental Condition is <u>the</u> Condition of all conditionally apparent conditions.

18. A living being—necessarily originating as a non-separate process, due to the universal interdependent cycle of conditional causes and effects—does not self-originate (or arise as a result of separate and independent self-causation). The idea of separate self-existence (as an independent "self"-entity, or quantifiable ego-"I") is an illusion, an everywhere common sign, evident in the human world, due to the universal absence of right understanding of conditional existence and

right knowledge (or tacit Realization) of the Transcendental nature of Reality and Truth. All ideas of the separateness, the independence, and the ultimate (or eternal) self-existence of the conditionally arising world (and all it contains) are ignorant (or wrongly "knowing") and rationally unsupportable thoughts. Likewise, the idea of the separateness, the independence, and the ultimate (or eternal) self-existence of any kind of quantifiable "self" (or ego-"I") is an ignorant (or wrongly "knowing") and rationally unsupportable thought.

19. All that arises conditionally and (thus and thereby) appears as the evident experience of anyone is, as such, merely an idea (or a conditional state of mind). Therefore, <u>all</u> conditional experience—because it is entirely a conditionally caused state of mind—is an illusion (or a cause of wrong "knowledge" of conditional existence, and a cause of egoic "self"-delusion, or the non-"knowing" of the Transcendental, or non-conditional, Condition of Reality and Truth). Thus, from wrong "knowledge", and from egoic "self"-delusion (or the absence of the tacit Realization of the Transcendental nature of Reality and Truth), all conditionally causative actions arise, and all results develop in time and space, in accordance with the positive or negative characteristics of the various states of mind (and of "self"-presumed "knowledge") that underlie and cause the actions themselves.

20. If the action-causing ideas in mind are brought under control—then action itself, and even the action-caused "things" of experience, are brought under control. This evidence—which can be readily demonstrated by anyone at all—<u>proves</u> that "things" (or the conditionally caused apparent experiences of forms, entities, functions, states, and worlds) have no separate and independent existence (or self-existence in, of, and as themselves). That is to say, even all conditionally arising (or caused) phenomena are of a non-separate nature—existing <u>only</u> in, of, and <u>as</u> the non-conditional Transcendental Condition of Reality and Truth.

21. In the case of everyone who is yet possessed in mind by action-causing ideas, desire and seeking control the life. All <u>such</u> living beings inhabit the mental darkness of the universal ocean of illusions—utterly unaware of the Self-Illuminated Truth of the inherently non-conditional (and acausal) nature of Reality itself. As long as the mind remains possessed by the absence of right knowledge, the darkness of wrong "knowledge" will yet cause the bondage to all causes and effects. Therefore, the idea of separate "things" and the idea of separate ego-"I" are the causes in mind that ceaselessly re-assert the appearance of conditional existence itself.

22. No one is able to transcend the oceanic mass of wrong "knowing", except by means of right-knowledge-<u>only</u>.

23. No one who is firmly established in right knowledge (tacitly Realizing the non-conditional Transcendental state of Reality and Truth), and who (thus and thereby) inherently rightly understands the conditional (and not self-existing) nature of the world, will any more cause wrong "knowing" in the heart, and mind, and life—or act wrong "knowing" in the world of seeming here some more.

IV

The Sixth Stage Transcendentalist Ways of Advaita Vedanta and Buddhism—And The Seventh Stage Acausal Reality-Way of Adidam

✤

An Essay by Avatar Adi Da Samraj

1.

Most Indian fourth, fifth, and/or sixth stage traditions indicate a conditional Yogic (or technical, and psycho-physical) "method" of "subjective" in-turning (or dissociative introversion) as a means to achieve the ultimate goal of practice. As such, all such traditions are associated with conditional efforts, based on identification with the body-mind-"self", and oriented toward seeking an "inner" absolute. Ramana Maharshi's sixth stage "method" (of "Self-enquiry") is an example of such a path—as are all other psycho-physically exercised and supported "methods" of the sixth stage of life and of the fourth and fifth stages of life. In all such cases, the idea of effort is a search for an immortal (or eternal) condition of "inner self" (or "atman").

Gotama Sakyamuni (called the "Buddha") taught that the "inner self" is merely conditional (or impermanent, merely "caused", entirely dependent, and non-Ultimate), just as is the body. Shankara's intention (and cultural mission) was (at the CE seventh-to-eighth-century beginning of the decline of Buddhism in India) to re-assert the ancient pre-Buddhist (or Vedic and Upanishadic) Hindu culture of insight and practice that, in Shankara's view, agreed with the classical Buddhist principle of the non-Ultimacy of the merely conditional (or psycho-physical) "self", but which was founded on Hindu traditional scriptures and traditional modes of Hindu logic. Thus, Shankara made intensive use of the practice of selective scriptural quotation, application of traditional Hindu rules of logic (both to assert and to refute propositions in argument), and methodical affirmation of principles of interpretation (or hermeneutics) to summarize the scriptures and traditions of Hinduism in the terms of Advaitic (or Non-dualistic) "idealism" (which agrees, in some of its key fundamentals, with some of the key fundamentals of the Buddhist "realism" current at and up to the time of Shankara).

In keeping with the ancient Hindu traditions of scriptural authority and "idealist" logic, Shankara did not describe a conditional Yogic (and, thus, merely psycho-physically based) path of turning toward "within", but, rather, a Way based on direct intuition of That Which Is Self-Evident <u>As</u> Prior Self-Intuition—or, that is to say, not the "inner self", or individual "atman", but the Self-Evident "Atman That <u>Is</u> Brahman" (or the "Real Self", Priorly Self-Evident <u>As</u> "Brahman", or the Intrinsically Self-Evident Transcendental and Intrinsically egoless Reality). Thus, Shankara defended a Hindu "idealist" teaching of "atman"-transcending (or intrinsically egoless) Transcendental Self, as compared to Gotama Sakyamuni's Buddhist "realist" teaching of "anatman" (or no-"self") and Transcendental egolessness (or "Nirvana")—but, in both cases, the "root"-assertion is that the presumed conditional "self" is not "a self", but only a conditional and temporary phenomenon, without a "root-substantiality" (or any discrete and independent self-existence).

The key difference between the tradition of Shankara and that of Gotama Sakyamuni is relative to the prescription for practice relative to the Realization of That Which Inherently Transcends the psycho-physical (or merely conditional) "self". That difference is, fundamentally, the difference between the logic of "idealism" (or of the a priori assertion of propositions as being self-evidently the case) and the logic of "realism" (or of the a posteriori assertion of propositions as being the case based on the progressive observation of facts that imply the rightness of the thereby derived proposition).

The Hindu tradition of "idealist" logic is more ancient—and, indeed, more fundamental—than the classical Buddhist logic based on "realism". That is to say, what is intrinsically self-evident prior to and independent of any "experiential" observation, calculation, or inference relative to conditionally arising phenomena (which are, themselves, always changing, and, thus, not self-evident) is more fundamental than (and, altogether, prior and senior to) what is not intrinsically self-evident (or what depends upon "experiential" observation, calculation, and inference relative to conditionally arising phenomena). Thus, the Ultimate practice advocated by Shankara (and which is based on direct intuition in response to scripturally-transmitted propositions of Priorly Self-Evident Truth) is more direct and more ancient than the practice advocated by Gotama Sakyamuni (which is a practice based on a gradual conviction developed by means of prescribed disciplines of psycho-physical "self"-observation).

In any case, the "Real Self" (or egoless Transcendental Reality-Condition) of Shankara (and of Advaita Vedanta) Is the "Nirvana" (or egoless Transcendental Reality-Condition) of Gotama Sakyamuni (and of Buddhism in general)—but stated in the "idealist" language of traditional Hinduism (or of the most ancient tradition of India), rather than in the "realist" language of the later (and "experimental observation") schools of Indian Buddhism.

Shankara taught a sixth stage Way that was, in fact, very significantly unlike most of the stream of practicing cultures that generally characterized the Hindu traditions current at and up to the time of Shankara, and as is otherwise indicated by the greater mass of traditional Hindu scriptures. Indeed, Shankara's Way of practice was a kind of "radical" (or "at-the-root") Way of practice—whereas even the Way of practice advocated by Gotama Sakyamuni was, by contrast, only "revolutionary" (because, while it also contradicted many of the traditions, schools, and "methods" of Gotama's time, it, nonetheless, proposed a "method" of conditionally-based seeking, rather than a Self-Evident Truth to be directly intuitively Self-Realized).

Shankara taught a <u>thoroughly</u> Non-dualistic Way of no inward-turning and of no conditional Yogic (or merely psycho-physically based) means—whereas the practicing cultures and scriptural traditions of Hinduism familiar to Shankara were, in general, dualistically and psycho-physically based. Thus, Shankara emphasized selective quotation of scriptural passages that were (at least arguably) Non-dualistic, and, furthermore, Shankara applied rules of logic and hermeneutics with such consistency, power, and authority that, in the context of a tradition based on living debate, Shankara's "radical" argumentation transformed (then, and from then on) at least the general philosophical context of the entire Hindu tradition.

The schools of Buddhism familiar to Shankara apparently included both the classical (or so-called Hinayana) and the later Mahayana (and, perhaps, also, the Tantric) varieties—and, indeed, the Mahayana schools of Buddhism familiar to Shankara would have included modes of propositional argument more in the mode of "idealism" than would have been evident in the schools associated with classical (or early) Buddhism. Nevertheless, all schools of Buddhism are, at root, founded on "realist"— or conditional-reality-based—reasoning. Consequently, all schools of Buddhism are (in relation to Hindu traditions in general) "heterodox" (or based on the non-acceptance of the priority and authority of traditional Hindu scriptures, and, instead, dependent upon "learning from experience"), and, also, all schools of Buddhism are thoroughly rooted in the context of "observable phenomena" and the function of "mind". In stark contrast to these characteristics common to all schools of Buddhism, not only are Shankara and the genuine schools of Advaita Vedanta "orthodox" (or accepting of the priority and authority of traditional Hindu scriptures), but, even more fundamentally and importantly, they are rooted always and only in the Truth That <u>Is</u> Self-Evident, and always immediately available to direct intuition (or tacit Self-Realization), Prior to any and all conditionally arising phenomena.

Thus, for example, whereas Shankara proposed direct intuition of the Self-Evident "Atman That Is Brahman", Gotama Sakyamuni proposed the discipline of constantly observing conditionally arising (or "cause-and-effect"-driven) phenomena (especially of the bodily-emotional-and-mental ego-"self"), until "Nirvana"—or subsequent Transcendental Reality-Realization. For Shankara, all psycho-physical disciplines are merely preparatory (and not "causative") to the eventual non-conditional reception and direct intuitive Realization of the Non-dual teaching. Shankara certainly understood the necessity of many kinds of disciplines of the body-mind-"self"—and Shankara required the demonstration of full maturity of devotion, "self"-discipline, and the impulse to Transcendental Realization before an individual could be accepted into the non-conditional practice of direct intuition of the Non-dual Truth. However, Shankara strictly declared that no psycho-physical discipline of any kind could be an actual "causative" means to Realize the Non-dual Truth. Therefore, in stark contrast to Shankara and the schools of Advaita Vedanta that remained true to Shankara's teaching, Gotama Sakyamuni and the schools of Buddhism in general (with few exceptions—such as the Sixth Patriarch of the Ch'an, or Zen, tradition) taught that certain prescribed disciplines and techniques were the necessary psycho-physical (and effectively "causative") means that lead to "Nirvanic" (or Transcendental and Non-dual) Realization.

Nevertheless, and apart from the fundamental difference I have just now indicated, both Shankara (and the sixth stage traditions of Hinduism altogether) and Gotama Sakyamuni (and the sixth stage traditions of Buddhism altogether) advocate the One and Same Ultimate Realization, whether at the beginning or at the end—and Which Is the egoless (or "Nirvanic", or Transcending-the-conditional-atman) Realization of the Non-dual (or always Prior and Indivisible) Transcendental Condition of "self" and "world".

Over time, many have (based on their own limiting associations with conditional patterning in the context of stages of life previous to the sixth) argued to the contrary of Shankara, and (on the basis of the same pre-sixth-stage-of-life biases) many have described Shankara's arguments as reductive, and even (again, without benefit of right understanding) as a kind of revision of Buddhism (or as crypto-Buddhism), but the Ultimate Transcendental propositions of Shankara (like the Ultimate Transcendental propositions of Gotama Sakyamuni, and others within the historical traditions of Buddhism) remain as Self-Evidently True propositions—not based on historical cultural interactions and dependencies, but, rather, based on the undeniable Self-Evidence of Reality Itself. Thus, and altogether, even though traditions of lesser (or conditional, and psycho-physically based) practice and conditionally-presumed Realization protest (and feel unduly criticized by) the thoroughly Non-dualistic assertions of Shankara, the conditional Yogic "methods" of the fourth, fifth, and (in some cases) sixth stage teachings of the general Hindu tradition are thoroughly criticized and subordinated to the Ultimate Transcendental Truth by the sixth stage traditions of Shankara's Advaita Vedanta—and, indeed, by the Ultimate (or, at last, Non-conditional) propositions of the sixth stage traditions of Buddhism.

There is, clearly, an element of uncompromised, pure sixth stage Non-dualism (or Advaitism) evident within the ancient Hindu (Vedic and Upanishadic) scriptures, and Shankara identified and argued the absoluteness of that dimension of the Reality-teachings of the Indian ancients. However, it is also clear that there were few teachers and schools of strict Non-dualism existing at or before the time of Shankara. Also, it can, with historical justification, be said that Shankara, and the sixth stage Non-dualistic schools of Advaitism that followed or (otherwise) preceded Shankara, fully successfully accomplished the assimilation (or even the transcending) of "realist" Buddhism within "idealist" Hinduism—or the ascendancy of Indian Non-dualist "orthodoxy" over Indian Transcendentalist (but, nonetheless, dualistically and conditionally based) "heterodoxy". In any case, both Shankara (with the totality of Indian Advaitism) and Gotama Sakyamuni (with the totality of Indian Buddhism) Ultimately (and equally) declared and demonstrated (in the Non-dualistically true sixth stage manner) the One and Same and Self-Evident Reality-Truth That Inherently Transcends all conditional and merely psycho-physical presumptions, declarations, and Realizations.

2.

The common (or mutually equivalent) teachings of both Advaitism (or Non-dualism, in the Indian traditions of Advaita Vedanta) and Buddhism include the fundamental (and universally verifiable) observation that the conventionally presumed conditional "self" (or ego-"I") has no discrete, substantial, independent, or metaphysically absolute existence—and, therefore, the conditional "self" (or conventionally presumed ego-"I") is not "a self". On this basis, the traditions of both Advaitism and Buddhism together assert—in the characteristically sixth stage manner—that, because the conventionally presumed conditional "self" is (both as body and as mind, or both as percept and as concept) not "a self", it is (like the "world") not-"self".

The essence of Transcendental Realization (or egoless Self-En-lightenment) in the traditions of Buddhism is the cessation (or intrinsic transcending) of "causation", or the freedom of no-suffering of "caused", or merely apparent and conditional, states and "objects" of "experience", or the cessation (or intrinsic transcending) of the (or any) conditional and "causative" identity (or "atman", or ego-"I").

The essence of Transcendental Realization (or egoless Self-En-lightenment) in the traditions of Advaitism is the Intrinsic Self-Apprehension (or Non-conditional Self-"Knowledge") of egolessness (or the cessation, or intrinsic transcending, of false identity), or the Intrinsic Self-Realization of freedom from all bondage to motions of "causation" (or conditionally effective activity, or karmic "cause-and-effect"), or the cessation (or intrinsic transcending) of the (or any) conditional and "causative" identity (or "atman", or ego-"I").

Therefore, the traditions of both Buddhism and Advaitism teach the Transcendental Way of no-ego (or no-"self", or "anatman"), or the Transcendental Way of the cessation (or intrinsic transcending) of "self"-identification with the (or any) conditional and "causative" agent (or conditional and "causative" identity, or "atman", or ego-"I").

Both Buddhism and Advaitism assert—in the characteristic sixth stage manner—that the "atman" (or conventionally presumed separate egoic "self") is (both as body and as mind, or both as percept and as concept) "anatman" (or not "a self", and, altogether, not-"self").

In the characteristic (and characteristically sixth stage) teaching-language of Buddhism, all that (apparently) arises conditionally (or in the context of "causes" and "effects") is not-"self". Thus, if "self"-identification with not-"self" ceases (or is, whether immediately or eventually, transcended), the Non-conditional Condition (or Intrinsic State) That Is Prior to all conditions, all "causes", all "effects", and all mere descriptions Is Self-Evident As Such.

Likewise, in the characteristic (and characteristically sixth stage) teaching-language of Advaitism, all that (apparently) arises conditionally (or in the context of "causes" and "effects") is not-"self". Thus, if (whether immediately or eventually) Intrinsic Self-Apprehension of the Intrinsically Self-Evident Self-Condition (or Intrinsic Self-Intuition of the Intrinsically egoless Self-Nature and Self-State) That Is Prior to all conditions, all "causes", all "effects", and all mere descriptions Is Self-Realized As Self-Evidently Such (Prior to all conditional, or "causative", or psycho-physical efforts, and, thus, Prior to all conditional Yogic efforts), all "self"-identification with not-"self" ceases (or is intrinsically Transcended).

Thus stated, it is clear that the apparent (historical) differences between the "idealist" sixth stage teaching-language of Advaitism and the "realist" sixth stage teaching-language of Buddhism are the evidence of cultural differences between two mutually-opposed teaching-languages of argumentation—especially in the competitive context of the historical meetings (or oppositions and "clashes") between representatives of the historically separate streams of Advaitic and Buddhist traditions.

The entire Great Tradition of humankind (comprising the paths and Ways of the global totality of humankind in the developmental context of the first six stages of life) is, in summary, a debate between traditions of <u>transcendence</u>.

The general stream of traditions (and progressive paths) of transcendence functions in the context of psycho-physical "self"-identity and of conditional Yogic (or merely psycho-physically based and psycho-physically exercised) seeking-efforts to transcend the psycho-physical evidence (and inherent limitations) of "experience" in the context (variously) of the first six (or developmental) stages of life. By contrast, the "idealist" traditions of sixth stage Transcendental Advaitism (or Advaita Vedanta) and the more "idealist" (or less "realist") sixth stage traditions of Buddhism (such as that of Nagarjuna, and of the schools of Ch'an, and Zen, and Dzogchen) have long proposed a (variously described) Way of intrinsic (rather than conditionally achieved) transcendence.

The traditional (historical) cultures of both Advaitism and Buddhism are always situated within the always primary context of "self"-surrender and obedience to the Realizer (or En-light-ened Master), and (on that basis) all such traditional cultures are always associated with prescriptive systems of practices that are intended to establish an attitude or disposition (of equanimity, and of free availability of energy and attention) that is inherently able to be unobstructedly combined with the teaching-arguments (and other transmission-means) of Ultimate transcendence. Those systems of prescriptive practices include various traditions of mind-purification and renunciation, which (variously) apply modes of either psycho-physical sublimation, or psycho-physical pacification, or psycho-physical asceticism. Nevertheless, regardless of the peculiarities of preliminary (or preparatory) or, otherwise, would-be-"causative" practice-culture and of modes of teaching-language and teaching-argumentation, the traditions of both Advaitism and Buddhism equally and always firmly assert that, Ultimately, Realization <u>Itself</u> Stands Prior to and independent of any and all conditional activity (and, thus, any and all previously applied psycho-physical, or conditional Yogic, "methods")—but, rather, Realization Itself <u>Is</u> Intrinsic Self-Apprehension of the Self-Evident and Intrinsically egoless Self-Nature, Self-Condition, and Self-State That <u>Is</u> Prior to all conditions, all "causes", all "effects", all of conditionally apparent "self", and all efforts (or actions) of a conditional (or psycho-physical) kind.

Thus, and on this basis, I Declare and always Affirm that the only-by-Me Revealed and Given seventh stage (Transcendental Spiritual and Self-Evidently Divine) Reality-Way of Adidam is the Final Completion and Perfect Fulfillment of the entire Great Tradition of the six developmental stages of humankind—and, most especially, the only-by-Me Revealed and Given seventh stage (Transcendental Spiritual and Self-Evidently Divine) Reality-Way of Adidam is the Final (or seventh stage) Completion and Perfect (or seventh stage) Fulfillment of all the sixth stage traditions, and, especially, those of Advaitism and of Buddhism.

3.

There is only <u>One</u> "Substantial" and "Essential" Reality—Which Is of an egoless, Acausal, Indivisible, and Transcendental Spiritual Nature, and of Which everything is a transparent (or merely apparent), and non-necessary, and inherently non-binding modification. Such is the only-by-Me Revealed and Given seventh stage Realization.

The seventh stage Realization <u>Is</u> the Divine Self-Realization of the Self-Nature, Self-Condition, and Self-State That <u>Is</u> Reality Itself.

The seventh stage Realization <u>Is</u> the Divine Self-Realization of the Intrinsic and Self-Evident egolessness, Non-separateness, Indivisibility, and Non-conditional Nature, Condition, and State of Reality Itself.

The seventh stage Realization <u>Is</u> the Divine Self-Realization of the Conscious Light That Intrinsically Self-Recognizes (and, moment to moment, specifically transcends) any and all apparent "objects".

The seventh stage Realization specifically (and moment to moment) Divinely Self-Recognizes any and all apparent "objects" to Be Not-"different", Not-an-"object", and <u>As</u> Self (rather than as not-"self").

The seventh stage Realization Divinely and Perfectly Self-Recognizes and Self-Transcends <u>both</u> egoic "self" (or psycho-physical and separate "subjectivity", or "self"-identity) <u>and</u> apparent "object" (or conditional "world")—In and <u>As</u> egoless Self, Consciousness Itself, Indivisible Conscious Light Itself, Reality Itself, and Self-Evident Real (Acausal) God.

The One ("Substantial", "Essential", Prior, and Non-conditional) Condition of conditions <u>Is</u> the "Bright" Conscious Light Itself, the egoless, Indivisible, and Acausal Divine Self-Nature, Self-Condition, and Self-State of all-and-All.

The language of the sixth stage traditions—with its (characteristically, Advaitic) references to "the Self", and its (characteristically, Buddhist) references to "the essence of mind", and so forth—suggests a "subjective" principle that is "causative" (or, in some traditions, merely and exclusively detached) relative to what is apparently "objective". This is why the error of exclusion (or, in some cases, of antinomian, or "self"-indulgent, behavioral abstractedness) is characteristic of the sixth stage traditions—even those (Advaitic and Buddhist) traditions that assert independence from psycho-physical efforts and supports.

The only-by-Me Revealed and Given seventh stage Realization is not founded on an exclusionary identification with what is "subjective" to the human being. The seventh stage Realization is the Realization of the Divine Self-Nature, Self-Condition, and Self-State of all-and-All—everything apparently "subjective", and everything apparently "objective". The "subjective" is not the "cause" of the "objective". The "subjective" and the "objective" are, equally, apparent modifications of the same egoless Acausal Indivisible Divine Reality.

The "radical" (or "at-the-root") "equivalence" of—or the Intrinsic, Prior, and Perfect Non-"difference" between—the "subjective" and the "objective" is a fundamental aspect of the Uniqueness of the only-by-Me Divinely Avatarically Self-Revealed seventh stage Reality-Revelation.

V

WHAT IS REQUIRED TO REALIZE THE NON-DUAL TRUTH?

The Controversy Between The Talking School and The Practicing School of Advaitism

❖

An Essay by Avatar Adi Da Samraj

Certain proponents of Advaitism (or of the Truth of Non-dualism), even some who may be genuine Realizers (but only in the sixth stage sense) of the Great Truth of Advaita Vedanta, generally represent or advocate what I call the "talking" school of Advaitism. That is to say, their contact with disciples is primarily one of conversation, and the process in which they engage their listeners is basically (and even exclusively) a matter of attendance to verbal argumentation. (And this emphasis on, or even confinement to, the verbal context of Advaitism stands in dramatic contrast to the real practicing Ordeal and deep meditative process that many "talking" school Teachers have endured as the context of their own sixth stage process of Advaitic Realization.[1])

There is even a kind of "Emperor's New Clothes" syndrome associated with the "talking" school. It is said that, yes, there are many practices (other than listening) that could be engaged, but such practices are only necessary for those who are immature (or whose minds are not yet ripe for the "Truth-Taking"). Few, of course, want to acknowledge their immaturity or unreadiness for the One Thing desired by all. Therefore, the proud listeners doggedly refuse to acknowledge the necessity of their own ego-transcending Ordeal of counter-egoic practice, and so they merely listen (again and again).

Unlike the "talking" school, the original tradition of Advaita Vedanta requires great preparations and real qualifications for the Advaitic (or Non-dualistic) Realization, and such preparations (or qualifications) include practical "self"-discipline, the development of a disinclination toward the search for (and attachment to) the conditional satisfactions associated with what I have Described as the first five stages of life, and the achievement of a clear-minded and profound motivation toward Transcendental Self-Realization. Indeed, only individuals who were thus prepared would, in the strictest traditional setting, be welcomed even to listen to (and to seriously "consider") an Advaitic Teacher's discourses on Transcendental Truth.

In any case, the practice of listening is traditionally called "sravana". All proponents (both traditional and modern) of the "talking" school tend to isolate (or idealize) this first (or initial) stage of the total process, and (thus) make it the Only "Method" (or the one and only context of possible Realization). And they (especially the modern proponents of the "talking" school) do not generally require the traditional preparations or qualifications (whether as a prerequisite or an eventual attainment) on the part of their listeners. (Even modern proponents of the original tradition, or what I call the "practicing" school, generally do not require the traditional preparations as a qualification for listening—but effective disciplines and real qualifications are expected to appear over time. There is a tradition that expects Advaitins to accept sannyasa, or the life of an unmarried, or socially detached, celibate—but the modern trend is to return to the classical orientation of the Upanishadic era,[2] which calls both sannyasins and householders, or even Tantric practitioners,[3] to the practice and the Realization of the Non-dualistic Way.)

The complete traditional process of "practicing" Advaitism goes on from the "talking" and listening stage of sravana to the advancing stages of manana (or profound examination of the Teaching arguments, to the point of hearing, or intuitive understanding) and nididhyasana (or deep contemplation, to the degree of true and stable Realization of Inherent Samadhi, or Inherent Identification with Consciousness Itself). Although the proponents of the "talking" school generally look for some kind of understanding (or hearing) to develop in their listeners, the great practice and the Great Realization associated with the traditional discipline of nididhyasana appear to be generally neglected (or even disdained) by them.

This distinction between the "talking" school (or Teachers of the "talking" school) and the "practicing" school (or Teachers of the "practicing" school) points to a basic controversy within the tradition of Advaitism. At least since the time of Shankara, both of these two schools (or interpretations of Advaitism) have existed.

The "talking" school generally attracts those who have a minimal capability for (or capable impulse toward) renunciation, Yogic (or Spiritual) discipline, and deep meditation, but who (otherwise) are habituated to constantly talk, listen, and think. The "discipline" and the "Realization" in the "talking" school (especially in its modern form) are generally minimal, weak, superficial, temporary, and merely mental (or intellectual)—and the "talking" school is (and has been) rightly criticized because of this.

The modern "practicing" school of Advaitism is clearly represented and advocated by Teachers such as Swami Gnanananda Giri[4] and (at least with some of His devotees) Ramana Maharshi. Such Teachers also "talk", and their disciples listen, but—in the case of aspirants who are taken seriously—real qualifications (including practical "self"-discipline) are expected (at least over time). Likewise, the Teachers of the "practicing" school clearly indicate that hearing (or fundamental understanding of Teaching arguments) is not itself Ultimate Enlightenment (or an end in itself), but it is only the beginning of practice (or the seed of Ultimate Enlightenment). Therefore, according to the Teachers of the "practicing" school, hearing must lead to right (and most profound) enquiry into (or direct Identification with) the Inherent and

Transcendental Self-Nature (or Perfectly Subjective Self-Condition) of the apparent conditional "subject" (or conditional "self")—Which Transcendental (or Perfectly Subjective) Self-Condition Inherently Transcends the apparent conditional "subject" (or conditional "self"). And such right enquiry necessarily (and spontaneously) becomes deep ("object"-transcending) meditation (or "dhyana"), and (at least eventually) "Jnana Samadhi" (or most profound, and thoroughly "object"-excluding, Identification with Consciousness Itself),[5] and (potentially) even sixth stage "Sahaja Nirvikalpa Samadhi",[6] which is the basis for the apparent premonitions (or partial intuitions and limited foreshadowings) of the only-by-Me Revealed and Given seventh stage of life that have sometimes been expressed within the traditional sixth stage schools, and which is a matter of deeply Abiding in the basically and tacitly "object"-excluding (and, thus, conditionally achieved) sixth stage Realization of the Transcendental Self-Condition, while otherwise naturally "experiencing" the natural arising of mental and physical "objects", and naturally allowing the performance of mental and physical activities. However, as I have Revealed, the necessary (but only preliminary, or sixth stage) Process is finally and Most Perfectly Fulfilled and Completed only in Divine Self-Awakening (or What I call "Open Eyes", or "seventh stage Sahaja Nirvikalpa Samadhi"),[7] Which Is utterly and inherently non-exclusive (and not conditionally Realized, but Nonconditionally, and Inherently, and Inherently Most Perfectly Realized) Transcendental, Inherently Spiritual, Intrinsically egoless, and Self-Evidently Divine Self-Realization and effortless (or Non-conditionally, and Inherently, and Inherently Most Perfectly Realized) Transcendental, Inherently Spiritual, Intrinsically egoless, and Self-Evidently Divine Self-Abiding—even (should they arise) in the apparent context of the arising of all conditional phenomena and all conditional (or psycho-physical) states, and always, spontaneously and Inherently (and Inherently Most Perfectly), Divinely Self-Recognizing all apparently arising conditional phenomena and conditional (or psycho-physical) states as transparent (or merely apparent), and non-necessary, and inherently non-binding modifications of the Transcendental, Inherently Spiritual, Intrinsically egoless, and Self-Evidently Divine Self-Nature, Self-Condition, Source-Condition, and Self-State Itself.

Some interpreters of the Teaching of Shankara propose (or may seem to propose) that Shankara Himself was an advocate (indeed, the chief proponent) of the "talking" school. According to one "point of view",[8] listening attentively to the "Mahavakyas", or the Upanishadic Principal Declarations (such as "Tat Tvam Asi", which means "That Thou Art"), or listening to the Great Upanishadic Truth as expounded by a Transcendentally Self-Realized Teacher (such as Shankara) is sufficient for (sixth stage) Realization (of the Inherent Samadhi of Consciousness Itself)—but Shankara did not (otherwise) propose (or dogmatically affirm) that listening to Teaching arguments (to the point of under-standing) is the only "Method" for such (sixth stage) Realization.[9]

Clearly, Shankara did affirm that listening could be sufficient for (sixth stage) Realization. Indeed, it is true that, in the case of some rare and uniquely prepared individuals, listening—particularly listening to a true Realizer, or listening to insight itself, however that insight may be communicated or originated—is sufficient for (sixth stage) Realization of the Inherent Samadhi of Consciousness Itself. The Awakening of Ramana Maharshi is a modern example of such sudden Realization. And, for some others, the Darshan (or seeing, or mere sighting) of a true Realizer is sufficient for such Realization.

However, Shankara clearly indicated that only exceptionally prepared individuals are qualified even to listen (or to practice sravana), and He (likewise) clearly indicated that only certain unique individuals (in whom the mind is no longer, effectively, a limit on the possibility of Inherent Samadhi) can (or will) Realize Inherent Samadhi directly and immediately via listening.

Shankara clearly indicated that a broad range of preparations are necessary before listening (to the Vedantic Great Truth) can be either appropriate or effective. Those necessary preparations include the development of the power of discrimination (particularly between the Real, or the Eternal or Permanent or Merely Existing, and the un-Real, or the conditional and temporary), the power of renunciation (or, as I have indicated, even the transcending of all purposes and results associated with the first five stages of life), the power of equanimity, and the motive-power of longing (for Liberation, or Freedom Itself). Likewise, Shankara clearly indicated that, even in the case of individuals specifically prepared in the manner described, the Inherent Samadhi of Consciousness Itself will not necessarily (or even likely) Awaken through sravana (or listening) alone—but the further stages of manana and nididhyasana will, in the general case, be necessary.

Thus, Shankara (in fact) Taught in the broad context of the "practicing" school. And, as indicated in various of Shankara's own original (or, otherwise, traditionally, or even recently, attributed) writings and commentaries,[10] Shankara even advocated (or, otherwise, approved) fourth and fifth stage practices as possible preparatory means—for removing (or, otherwise, transcending) apparent obstructions to sixth stage Realization.

Shankara Himself intuitively Realized the inherently actionless (or Transcendental) Brahman (or Consciousness Itself). He did not affirm (as Ultimate Reality) the mere (and exclusive, or individual) atman (the "soul"—or the separate, but permanent, "self"-entity), but He Realized that what is conventionally (or previous to Realization) presumed to be the atman (or the "soul", or the separate conscious "self") Is (Inherently, and by virtue of Realization) Only Self-Existing and Self-Radiant Transcendental Consciousness Itself (or Brahman). However, Most Ultimate (or Inherently Most Perfect) Enlightenment Is <u>Only</u> That Realization and Demonstration That <u>Is</u> Absolute Freedom—Self-Existing and Self-Radiant As Consciousness Itself, All (and Infinite As) Love-Bliss. And <u>That</u> is no small matter or state of mind, but It <u>Is</u> What (Ultimately) <u>Is</u>—and That Is (Truly Most Ultimately, and Inherently Most Perfectly) Revealed Only By (or In the Shine Of) the Inherently Most Perfect (and by-Divine-Grace-Given) Sacrifice (or the Inherently Most Perfect, and by-Divine-Grace-Given, transcending) of the conditional "self". At last, Only This Most Ultimate (or Inherently Most Perfect) Realization Truly, Finally, Completely, and Most Perfectly Reveals The Inherently One (and Inherently Real Acausal) God, or Great (Obvious, or Always Already) Truth, or Ultimate (or Inherently Perfect) Reality. That Most Ultimate (or Inherently Most Perfect) Realization Is Unique to the only-by-Me Revealed and Demonstrated and Given seventh stage of life and to the only-by-Me Revealed and Demonstrated and Given Reality-Way of Adidam. And Only That Most Ultimate (or Inherently Most Perfect and Complete) Realization, Awakened and Demonstrated, can Finally Fulfill (or Most Perfectly Complete and End) the human Ordeal.

VI

TEN DECLARATIONS OF THE TRANSCENDENTAL SELF-IDENTITY OF CONSCIOUSNESS ITSELF

The Reality-Teachings of The Advaitic Sage Shankara

From the Dasasloki, *traditionally attributed to Shankara, the principal Master-Sage at the origin of the Advaitic (non-dualist) tradition*

The Dasasloki *(literally "Ten Declarations") is a short work consisting of ten verses. Although tradition ascribes the work to Shankara, the authorship of the work is unclear. According to Madusudhana Sarasvati's biography of Shankara, these verses were spoken by a youthful Shankara after approaching his Guru for instruction. His Guru allegedly asked Shankara the question, "Who are you?" Shankara's reply, in the form of this text, highlights what the tradition regards as the quintessence of Advaita Vedanta, setting forth the true nature of the Transcendental Condition, which is senior to the three principal states of human experience (waking, dreaming, and sleeping).*

FIRST DECLARATION

What is not always already the case is not the Consciousness of it. What arises, changes, and passes away in the view of Consciousness is not the Consciousness <u>itself</u>. What is an "object" of Consciousness is not Consciousness itself. All conditionally arising "objects", states, causes, and effects—all conditions, and all combinations of conditions—arise, change, and pass away. All that is merely conditionally the case is not always already the case. What appears to be the case from the "point of view" of one state (such as waking, or dreaming), but which would not appear to be the case from the "point of view" of another state (such as deep sleep), is not always already the case. Any state of experience that is, itself, not always already the case is not the Consciousness (or the Transcendental Identity) of it. Only That which is intrinsically and Self-Evidently the case—prior to all that is merely conditional, "objective", or not always already the case—<u>is</u> always already the case. I <u>am</u> only the intrinsically Self-Evident Transcendental Self-Identity—Which <u>is</u> Consciousness <u>itself</u>.

SECOND DECLARATION

The "I" of conditionally arising "self"-identity is not always already the case. The "I" of conditional experiencing and conditional knowing is merely a convention of conditionally arising mind. The "I" of speech-mind is an uninspected thought, which, upon inspection, is found to have no known (or specifically indicated) referent. The "I"-thought is merely an "object", conditionally arising and changing and passing away in the ever-changing flow of states, conditions, and "objects" that are not always already the case. Neither the "I" nor its apparent conditions, "objects", and states are Consciousness itself. I am not the "I" that arises conditionally. I am not the associations (or states, conditions, and "objects") of the "I" that arises conditionally. I am not the body or the mind. I am not any state of body or mind. I have no conditional status, no stage of development, and no definable identity. There is no effort of body or mind whereby I may attain or Realize my intrinsically Self-Evident Identity. Even all the Yogic methods of concentration, meditation, and contemplative absorption cease to apply to me when only my intrinsically Self-Evident Identity is understood and directly Self-Apprehended. I am only the intrinsically Self-Evident Transcendental Self-Identity—Which is Consciousness itself.

THIRD DECLARATION

No relations, no things, no "God"-ideas, no holy books, no ritual acts, no sacred places, and not even the cosmic world itself are there, in the state of deep sleep. No "I" arises there, in the state of deep sleep. Nevertheless, even if no "I" is thought and no "object" of any kind arises—as in the state of deep sleep—Consciousness itself is always already (intrinsically and Self-Evidently) the case. I am only the intrinsically Self-Evident Transcendental Self-Identity—Which is Consciousness itself.

FOURTH DECLARATION

There is no idea—or any philosophy, or any religious doctrine, or any verbal definition at all—that is Consciousness itself. Indeed, no ideas, or philosophies, or religious doctrines, or verbal definitions of any kind are relevant—or have any application, or any causative relationship, or even any necessity at all—in, or as a means to Self-Apprehend, Consciousness itself. The inherent purity—or "objectlessness", or relationlessness, or non-differentiated Self-Characteristic—of Consciousness (itself) is absolute and perfect. I am only the intrinsically Self-Evident Transcendental Self-Identity—Which is Consciousness itself.

FIFTH DECLARATION

Consciousness (itself) is not above, not below, not inside, not outside, not in between, not at the center, not at the periphery, not opposite, not other, and not different. Consciousness (itself) is everywhere and nowhere, one and only, prior to all and (yet) pervading all, as the single "substance" (or substratum and Self-Condition) of all. Consciousness (itself) is inherently indivisible, non-conditional, and non-different. I am only the intrinsically Self-Evident Transcendental Self-Identity— Which is Consciousness itself.

SIXTH DECLARATION

Consciousness (itself) is not an "object" to itself. Consciousness (itself) is without visibility, or form of any kind. Consciousness (itself) is colorless, shapeless, and without dimensions, stages, levels, or measures of any kind. Consciousness (itself) is neither large nor small, neither short nor long, neither brief nor long-lasting, and neither of the nature of space nor of the nature of time. Consciousness (itself) is Self-radiant and without "point of view". Consciousness (itself) is all-pervading, like light—but light itself is a mere subordinate of the Consciousness to Which (and in Which) it appears. I am only the intrinsically Self-Evident Transcendental Self-Identity—Which is Consciousness itself.

SEVENTH DECLARATION

In Consciousness (itself), there is neither "you" nor "I", neither separate "self" nor separate other. The intrinsically Self-Evident Self-Awareness of Consciousness itself contains no opposites or differences of any kind. I am only the intrinsically Self-Evident Transcendental Self-Identity— Which is Consciousness itself.

EIGHTH DECLARATION

Consciousness (itself) is the mere (or inherently actionless, inherently formless, inherently non-separate, and inherently non-different) witness of all conditionally arising "objects", conditions, and states. Consciousness (itself) is not of the nature of the waking state, the dream state, or the state of deep sleep. Consciousness (itself) is, as it were, a fourth state—not defined or limited by the three conditionally apparent states (of waking, dreaming, and deep sleep). I <u>am</u> only the intrinsically Self-Evident Transcendental Self-Identity—Which <u>is</u> Consciousness <u>itself</u>.

NINTH DECLARATION

Consciousness (itself) is Self-existing, always already Self-established, not caused, not conditional, not dependent. The entire conditionally apparent cosmic universe is conditionally arising, not always already the case, consisting entirely of mutually dependent conditions and dualistic oppositions, altogether in a perpetual flux of relations of cause and effect. Consciousness (itself) <u>is</u> Reality <u>itself</u>—one, only, Self-existing, Self-radiant, and always already the case. The conditionally apparent cosmic universe of things and others that come and go is <u>not</u> Reality <u>itself</u>—but only a conditional and dependent appearance <u>within</u> Reality itself (Which <u>is</u> Consciousness itself). I <u>am</u> only the intrinsically Self-Evident Transcendental Self-Identity—Which <u>is</u> Consciousness <u>itself</u>.

TENTH DECLARATION

Consciousness (itself) is not even best described as "one"—for how could there be a second, or anything at all, different from Consciousness itself (such that Consciousness is, itself, different from that)? Consciousness (itself) is not any characteristic or condition relative to which there can be an opposite, or an other, or a contrasting anything at all. Consciousness (itself) is perfectly non-dual—not divisible, not differentiated, and not different. How can Truth be said to be of shape or size? What is the limit of limitlessness? What is the measure of the immeasurable? What is the definition of the indefinable? Truth <u>is</u> Consciousness <u>itself</u>—the intrinsically Self-Evident Transcendental Self-Identity of one and all and everything. I <u>am</u> That.

VII

THE FIVE DECLARATIONS OF ULTIMATE KNOWLEDGE

The Reality-Teachings of The Advaitic Tradition As A Whole, On The Necessary Characteristics of An Inherently Perfect Guru, or True Master-Sage

From the Maneesha Panchakam

Maneesha Panchakam *(or "Five Verses on Wisdom") is another text traditionally ascribed to Shankara, which he is said to have spoken when confronted by the God Siva in the guise of an untouchable who taught Shankara about Non-duality. The verses themselves contain no attribution of authorship and, thus, likely represent a vision of Reality and the Nature of the Transcendental Self as understood in the Advaita Vedanta tradition which followed Shankara.*

THE FIRST DECLARATION OF ULTIMATE KNOWLEDGE

Consciousness (itself) is the one Reality and Truth.

The First Elaboration of the Necessary Characteristics of an Inherently Perfect Guru, or True Master-Sage

"Reality is Consciousness itself—not any apparent 'object' of Consciousness itself. The Truth of Consciousness (itself) is that it is one, indivisible, not caused, unchanging, eternal, and all-pervading—whereas 'objects' are many, countless, conditionally caused, mutually opposed, always changing, and temporary. The intrinsic Self-Condition of Consciousness is that it is the mere (or inherently actionless) witness of the entire cosmic universe (of causes, effects, and 'objects') and of all conditionally arising states (of waking, dreaming, and deep sleep)." Only one who is a Realizer of this Self-Confession of the Reality, the Truth, and the intrinsic Self-Condition of Consciousness <u>itself</u> is an inherently perfect Guru, or true Master-Sage.

The Second Declaration of Ultimate Knowledge

I <u>am</u> Consciousness itself, the one Reality and Truth.

The Second Elaboration of the Necessary Characteristics of an Inherently Perfect Guru, or True Master-Sage

"I am <u>only</u> Consciousness itself—one, indivisible, Self-existing prior to the cosmic universe and all conditional states, and Self-radiant as all-pervading Bliss. The entire cosmic universe arises as a seeming appearance (of conditional causes, effects, and 'objects')—made apparent by an non-necessary (and merely apparent, or illusory) torsion of centrifugal, centripetal, and neutral tendencies of motion within the matrix of Bliss, or Self-Light, that is the Self-radiance of Self-existing Consciousness itself. No matter what seems to arise <u>thus</u> (as an apparent 'objective' super-imposition on Consciousness itself), I <u>am</u> only Consciousness <u>itself</u>—

Self-radiant <u>as</u> non-conditional Bliss <u>itself</u>." Only one who is a Realizer of this Self-Confession of the Identity and State of Consciousness <u>itself</u> is an inherently perfect Guru, or true Master-Sage.

THE THIRD DECLARATION OF ULTIMATE KNOWLEDGE

Every conditionally apparent being, and even the entire conditionally apparent cosmic universe, is only Consciousness itself, the one Reality and Truth.

THE THIRD ELABORATION OF THE NECESSARY CHARACTERISTICS OF AN INHERENTLY PERFECT GURU, OR TRUE MASTER-SAGE

"Every conditionally apparent being, and even the entire conditionally apparent cosmic universe, merely apparently (and without ultimate necessity) arises, changes, and disappears in conditionally apparent space and time. Consciousness itself is the Self-existing and Self-radiant matrix of this conditional apparition of beings, things, and events. If mere Self-Abiding <u>as</u> Consciousness itself is established, the mind is dissolved in its Source-Condition, the body is rested (thereby) in the Self-radiant Bliss of Consciousness itself, and the exercises of desire and seeking that have caused the present embodiment are inherently and perfectly transcended." Only one who is a Realizer of this Self-Confession of ultimate knowledge—based upon the contemplation of That which, <u>alone</u>, <u>is</u> ultimate knowledge—is an inherently perfect Guru, or true Master-Sage.

THE FOURTH DECLARATION OF ULTIMATE KNOWLEDGE

Consciousness <u>itself</u>—intrinsically Self-existing prior to all mental and sensory "objects", and inherently Self-radiant as Bliss itself—is Self-Evident as the true and very Self-Condition of <u>all</u> beings.

THE FOURTH ELABORATION OF THE
NECESSARY CHARACTERISTICS OF AN INHERENTLY PERFECT
GURU, OR TRUE MASTER-SAGE

"All beings are always already Self-Awake and Self-Illumined by Consciousness itself, even though Consciousness (itself) may yet be apparently obscured by the 'objects' and tendencies of body and mind—much as the sun may be temporarily obscured from view by a visible thickness of clouds." Only one who "Locates" the Self-Evident State of Self-Illumination that is Consciousness itself—and who, by Self-Abiding as That, Realizes and Self-Confesses this ultimate knowledge of the Self-existing and Self-radiant Self-Condition of Consciousness itself—is an inherently perfect Guru, or true Master-Sage.

THE FIFTH DECLARATION OF ULTIMATE KNOWLEDGE

Consciousness itself is the infinite and inexhaustible ocean of Bliss, in which all beings may Realize perfect Happiness.

THE FIFTH ELABORATION OF THE
NECESSARY CHARACTERISTICS OF AN INHERENTLY PERFECT
GURU, OR TRUE MASTER-SAGE

"The mind is perfectly dissolved—or Realized to be inherently non-existent—if the Self-radiant Bliss of Self-existing Consciousness itself is known. That ocean of Bliss is (itself) the one and only ultimate knowledge. Therefore, one who Realizes ultimate knowledge does not merely 'know' the one Reality and Truth. Rather, one who Realizes ultimate knowledge is (thus and thereby) the one Reality and Truth." Only one who thus Realizes and Self-Confesses ultimate knowledge is an inherently perfect Guru, or true Master-Sage. An inherently perfect Guru, or true Master-Sage, should be worshipped with true devotion by one and all—for ultimate knowledge is a Way and a Realization Given (and made possible for all) <u>only</u> by means of the Blessing-Grace of an inherently perfect Guru, or true Master-Sage.

Epilogue: The Three "Dispositions" of the Comprehensive Practice That Becomes the Perfect Realization of Ultimate Knowledge

I. The Orientation of Practice Based Upon the "Disposition" of Identification With the Body:

"Based upon the 'disposition' of identification with the body, I am the devotee-servant of the bodily apparent Person of my inherently perfect Guru—the true Master-Sage to whom my body and mind are constantly surrendered."

II. The Orientation of Practice Based Upon the "Disposition" of Identification With the Mind:

"Based upon the 'disposition' of identification with the mind, I am like an idea, yielding toward devotional unity (or re-union) with the infinite Spiritual matrix (or ascended Bliss-Mind) of my inherently perfect Guru—the true Master-Sage to whom my body and mind are constantly surrendered."

III. The Orientation of Practice Based Upon the "Disposition" of the Intrinsically Self-Evident Self-Condition That <u>Is</u> Consciousness Itself:

"Based upon the 'Disposition' of Intrinsic Self-Identification with Consciousness <u>itself</u>, I am not separated from the Self-existing and Self-radiant State of my perfectly Self-Realized Guru. Therefore, by means of the ego-surrendering exercise of non-difference, my devotion is perfectly maintained, and I need only Self-Abide in the ultimate knowledge of the Heart-Current of Bliss, in which I am constantly Blessed to be Awake by the Compassionate Regard of my inherently perfect Guru—the true Master-Sage to whom my body and mind are constantly surrendered."

VIII

MY RENDERINGS OF THE ANCIENT
REALITY-TEACHINGS

✢

*A Discourse Given by Avatar Adi Da Samraj to
His devotees, on January 28, 2006—directly after He had
first Recited His Renderings of the Reality-Teachings
of Gotama Sakyamuni and Nagarjuna*

1.

It should be clear from My Renderings of the traditional texts in this book that there is no difference between the Teachings of Truth that are contained in the Reality-Teachings of Buddhism and the Teachings of Truth that are contained in the Reality-Teachings of Advaitism.

The traditions of Buddhism and Advaitism have often argued among themselves, and they have, historically, propagandized themselves in human society by seeming to be in conflict with one another. In this manner, differences have been indicated that do not exist in Reality. For example, the Buddhist doctrine of "anatta" (or "no-self") is said by some to be a counter-argument to the Teaching of Advaitism, intended to suggest (in direct opposition to the argument of Advaitism) that there is no Transcendental (or Non-conditional) Condition (or egoless Self-Nature, or what later Buddhists, such as Nagarjuna, would indicate by the term "Buddha-Nature"). However, the original Teachings attributed to Gotama Sakyamuni Himself state plainly that, if there were no Non-conditional Condition, no Transcendental Self-Condition, then there would be no possibility of Liberation. In other words, if all there is is conditionality, there cannot be any Liberation from conditionality.

The suggestion (or argument) that is propagandized by certain Buddhist proponents—as if declaring that there is no Transcendental Self-Condition—is (itself) simply a strategic device in the realm of philosophy, or, that is to say, propaganda meant to "win" (or intended to present the "other" as an opponent, and to draw people to the side of one tradition as opposed to another). The Truth that is associated with the Reality-Teachings of Buddhism is exactly the same Truth that is associated with the Reality-Teachings of Advaitism. It is the Truth of Reality Itself, the Truth That Is Reality Itself—Which is Non-conditional, Transcendental, and Acausal in Nature. You will find that the traditional texts in this book, both the Buddhist and the Advaitist texts, are speaking about exactly the same Transcendental Realization. Each of those traditions has, historically, communicated through propagandistic arguments relative to the other—but only because of the divisive nature of institutional and cultural provincialism and competitiveness. Ultimately, there is no justification for the conflict whatsoever.

Thus, in My Divine Avataric Person and My Divine Avataric Reality-Teaching, there are no distinctions made between these two traditions. In fact, I propose them to you as the historical traditions in most direct continuity with My Divine Avataric Revelation of the Reality-Way of Adidam. When the language of propaganda—of interpretation, of opposition, of mummed "difference"—is eliminated from the texts of the Buddhist tradition and from the texts of the Advaitic tradition, they speak as if spoken by one person. And now I have Spoken them— in My Own and Indivisible Person, and in My Own and Single Voice. And, Thus Spoken, they are a single and indivisible tradition.

Of course, each of these traditions contains various limitations that are associated with the stages of life, including limitations that are associated with the characteristic error of the sixth stage of life in particular. Nevertheless, as I have Said to you, these traditions are not wrong because of their sometimes not-yet-perfect indications. Rather, the yet limited Teachings of these traditions should, rightly, be understood to be preliminary Teachings or preparatory practices. Such Teachings are limited in that sense—in the sense that they are preliminary (or preparatory) to the Demonstration of Most Perfect Realization, rather than in the sense that they are "wrong".

There are utterances in these traditions that are "wrong" (or false). There are "wrong" views. Yet, the "wrong" views are not spoken by Me in My Renderings of these texts. Rather, these texts, as I have presented them to you, speak in a manner that shows the utter compatibility of the two traditions, of Buddhism and Advaitism. There is not the slightest inherent difference between the Truth that one is proclaiming and the Truth the other is proclaiming—not the slightest.

Nevertheless, these traditions speak within the context of the first six (or developmental) stages of life, most particularly in the mode of the sixth stage of life. Therefore, there is more that had yet to be Revealed. A Completing Utterance had yet to be made. That Completing Revelation is the Unique Nature of My seventh stage Divine Avataric Reality-Teaching. The reader of the Texts of *Eleutherios* and *The Lion Sutra*[1] is Given Reality-Teaching that is free of the limitations of the first six stages of life and that is in the mode of the seventh stage (or Nonconditional) Realization of Reality Itself. My Divine Avataric Reality-Teaching is a Completion of the traditional Buddhist and Advaitist Teachings (and even all other sixth stage, or, altogether, first-six-stages-of-life, Teachings)—and, therefore, It is Continuous with them (and with even all traditions of the One Great Tradition of humankind as a whole).

The translating of traditional texts tends to be strategic. Translated texts speak in accordance with the degree of understanding of those who translate and present the texts. Sectarian translations, and even some texts themselves (in their original language), also speak with the intention to propose differences argumentatively. Thus, for these reasons, translations of traditional texts (and, also, some texts originally, even previous to translation into non-original languages) are often largely incomprehensible—encumbered with peculiarities, strategic intentions, and the intention to be different from something else that is being argued against, and (altogether) encumbered by ordinary mind (the ordinary mind of those making the texts originally and/or those making the translations).

Oddly enough, the renderings of traditional sacred texts are, most often, not made by Realizers—particularly in the modern day. In fact, to be involved in any kind of "religious" or Spiritual practice—not to mention having Realized on that basis—is regarded (at least in the conventional academic context) as a kind of fault. It is presumed (in the conventional academic realm) that translators of sacred texts must (ideally, or, otherwise, professionally) be detached from the subject of "religion", Spirituality, and Transcendental practice—dissociated from it, not committed to it, not involved in it, not really in any way even affected by it—such that they exist in some kind of "objective purity" that gives them the unique capability, somehow or other, to translate the text rightly and truly. It is presumed (in the conventional academic realm) that your bonafides must be, typically, those of the realm of scholarly endeavor, and those bonafides (more or less characteristically) require non-practice and non-Realization—the kind of qualifications that might be said to belong in the realm of science (wherein, characteristically, there is the presumption of a systematic and strategic "objectification" of subject matter).

However, the Truth of Reality is not Realizable on such a merely "objective" basis. The Reality-Teachings of Gotama Sakyamuni and Nagarjuna, included herein, speak directly to this matter of presumed "objectification", and to the illusions that arise through "objectification", and to the mind that merely "objectifies" phenomena (including the phenomenal "self"). Gotama Sakyamuni and Nagarjuna both examine the "self"-deluded habit of "objectivity", that declares phenomenal appearances to be "a separate this, that, or the other thing—inherently independent of any other thus separate this, that, or the other thing".

Their "detachment" required participatory engagement, and not mere non-participatory "objectivity". Likewise, their discipline was based upon a fundamental impulse toward the transcending (and even the dissolution) of the ego-"I" (or separate "self")—not an impulse toward the achievement of ego-power over conditionally arising phenomena themselves (whether by means of "knowledge" or any other conditional achievement, and not even by means of "detachment" itself). Thus, it was understood, even anciently, that precisely that non-participatory and ego-based "objectivity" which has now become the ordinary basis for "knowledge", discourse, learning, culture, and politics in the common "world" is utterly false—self-deluded and "self"-bound (and a reinforcer of "self"-delusion and "self"-bondage).

To "objectify" sacred texts by detaching oneself from participation in both their essential discipline and their potential Realization, and, on that basis, to attempt to translate or interpret them, is to commit the very error that is principally addressed in the texts themselves. Therefore, most rightly, someone who translates (or re-speaks, or, otherwise, interprets or explains) traditional Reality-Teachings should have <u>utterly</u> submitted his or her life to the essential practice associated with Realization <u>and</u> should (thereby) have come to the point of Realization.

The traditional texts presented by Me in this book are only a few in number, but they are outstanding among the most important texts ever written. They are so much to the point that they are profoundly Illuminating—not sufficient for the Awakening of Transcendental Realization Itself, but potentially sufficient to bring anyone to practice at the feet of a true Master.

The true (and truly effective) Reality-Teaching of Truth Itself is (inherently) profoundly Illuminating, and always (unambiguously) to the point—and it must be rightly and precisely communicated, if it is to be fully received by one who is truly prepared to receive It. Reality-Instruction, as directly Given by a true Realizer, is not convoluted and ambiguous. Therefore, in making these Renderings, I have Worked to

Speak these traditional texts plainly, such that their inherent power of Illumination can be felt by anyone truly prepared for the listening. In My Renderings of these traditional texts, they are all Spoken in a manner that is always precise and entirely to the point. There are not an infinite number of points being made in these particular texts. The Reality-Instruction they communicate is very direct and basic.

What you will receive of any form of Reality-Instruction depends on your preparedness, and on your disposition (altogether). What you will do about all of this depends on your response to Me.

2.

DEVOTEE: Great Divine Lord, Adi Da, not a single person here in this room today could doubt that You are the Master of the Great Tradition of humankind. Today, again, so perfectly, and as we have always seen in all these years with You, You have Championed the Great Tradition, You have Purified it, You have Served it, and You have Served the mind of all beings—not just with Your Words, and with Your Person, but with Your Divine Prescience as well, because You have already Addressed the very question that I came to discuss with You, which is this matter of the presumed controversies, conflicts, and differences between Hinduism and Buddhism.

AVATAR ADI DA SAMRAJ: You are bringing up the matter of the conflict between Buddhism and what is now called "Hinduism" (as an entire, and complex, tradition)—whereas I have, in particular, been Speaking of the traditions of Buddhism and Advaitism. The tradition of Advaitism first appeared, historically, <u>within</u> (and as a part of) the culture of what is now called "Hinduism"—whereas Buddhism, while also originating in India, was, from its beginning, based upon principles and motives that did not depend upon or, otherwise, appeal (or resort) to the traditional authorities of what is now called "Hinduism". <u>That</u> is the reason for the presumed difference between Buddhism and Advaitism.

There is no inherent difference between the Realization of Shankara and the Realization of Nagarjuna and Gotama Sakyamuni. Yet, there were institutional differences between Buddhism and Hinduism—and those differences "required" a conflict and a victory.

It is often pointed out that Buddhism virtually disappeared from India, even though it originated there. However, it could also be said that the tradition of Advaitism (or of Advaita Vedanta) is the "replacement" for Buddhism in Hindu India. Shankara argued His Advaitic Reality-Teachings by appealing to the authority of the traditional texts of Hinduism—principally the Upanishads, the *Bhagavad Gita,* of course the Vedas, and, also, the *Brahma Sutras*[2]—because those texts had to be defended in the face of the Buddhist "challenge" to Hindu philosophy. Buddhism, in contrast, was not identified with (nor did it appeal, or resort, to) such scriptural authorities, nor was Buddhism identified with (or appealing, or resorting, to) the institutional authorities (or the tradition of priesthood and temples) that was entrenched in the larger society that is now called "India". For this reason, Buddhism was regarded to be a kind of "alien" (or "heterodox") influence—and, therefore, the "orthodox" authorities of Hinduism had to be brought to bear in order to defeat this "alien" influence. Thus, there is a level of propaganda in the tradition of Advaita Vedanta that is specifically intended to counter the ideas of Buddhism.

Likewise, the tradition of Buddhism, which has largely flourished outside India (generally, elsewhere in Asia), has magnified its arguments that seem to be in opposition to traditional Hinduism and the traditional (scriptural and institutional) authorities of Hinduism. In both cases, there was an entrenched culture—on the one hand, Hinduism in India, and, on the other hand, a culture (Buddhism) which had nothing to do with the culture of Hinduism but which was becoming otherwise institutionalized, and which (over time) became entrenched elsewhere (outside India).

Such cultural or nationalistic conflicts—which supported the vast enterprises of institutions that were the foundations of the political domain and the economic domain—produced the necessity for a kind of warfare of propaganda between Buddhism and Hinduism, or even between Buddhism and Advaita Vedanta. "Advaitism" is simply a term for referring to the essential Truth of Reality—the Non-dual, Non-conditional Truth of Reality. Similarly, "Buddhism" is based on more than a name for Gotama Sakyamuni, but it is a term that indicates the State of Illumination that is associated with the Inherent Nature of Reality Itself.

As expressions of Truth, Buddhism and Advaitism have no inherent institutional associations. Truth Itself has no home-culture, no nation, nothing to defend. Therefore, when Buddhism and Advaitism, as traditions of actual Truth-Realization, come together in a room, there are no inherent differences between them. There is no inherent requirement that there be a cultural war, that there be a winner—and, in fact, there should be no winner, there can be no winner, and there is no winner. These traditions are talking about the same Reality, the Truth of Reality Itself—through the language of different traditions, yes, but (essentially) discoursing about the same matters.

Therefore, if true Buddhist Sages (or Realizers in the mode of Buddhism) and true Advaitic Sages (or Realizers in the mode of Advaitism) had simply met together somewhere, they would not (on the basis of Truth Itself) have invented the conflict that characterizes the culturally-invented differences between those two traditions in the public (or common) domain. The apparent differences between true Realizers themselves are made only by the characteristic uniqueness of individual true Realizers themselves, and, therefore, they are not matters of inherent conflict—if Reality Itself Shows Its Self-Evident Truth to and by means of each such one. Unlike the case of true Realizers themselves, the culturally-invented differences that are erected between institutions are made into devices of conflict—a conflict that is fought out only in places where cultural wars are assumed to be required. The differences between mere institutions are the seeds of ignorantly invented (and fundamentally Truthless) human conflict—and all of it is entirely of an egoic origin.

Buddhism, such as it was originally presenting itself, was simply not appealing (or resorting) to Vedic authority and the traditional texts that were regarded to be the basis of authority within the ancient culture of Hinduism. Therefore, Shankara (among others) argued the Advaitic Truth by appealing to the verity of the scriptures of Hinduism, thereby declaring their authority to be intact and the very basis for the Truth that He was communicating. His argument made Advaita Vedanta acceptable as a mode of Hinduism. As a result, Buddhism was (essentially) excluded, and, thus, it became peripheral in Hindu India.

There needed to be a cultural war only because there were institutions which could not make room for one another, which could not become a single (or unified) tradition. Therefore, in Truth, there is no conflict between true Buddhism and true Advaitism. There is no conflict whatsoever—only different terminologies and different "methods".

One can observe in My Renderings of the Teachings presented in these texts that they are speaking in common and "in the same room", and that (therefore) there is no basis for a conflict between them. They all fit into this book. They all fit in the Room with Me, because I need not defend Hinduism or Buddhism or anything else—not anything Western, nor anything Eastern, nor anything of a nationalistic nature. I have no inherited "religion" to defend. I have no "tribe". By having no such affiliation, I can Speak plainly, in terms of the non-difference between these traditions of Realization.

What there is of apparent difference is only in the traditional cultural wars that originated within the institutional and political circumstances wherein the two traditions came into "worldly" conflict.

In any case, it is not really the "Truths" of the "religions" themselves that are in conflict. It is not the true Saints and Realizers of the many and various traditions of humankind that are shouting angrily at one another from their separate rooms. Rather, the apparent conflict is always political—made by the identification of "religions" with institutions, with separate cultures, with nations, with political movements, and even with separate languages. The particular conflict between

Buddhism and Hinduism is, therefore, very political, as is all conflict in general. Conflict is all the "neighborhood-wars"[3] of egoity.

All of that has nothing whatsoever to do with the matter of Truth. Conflict is false—utterly false, unworthy, and destructive. Therefore, there is really no conflict between Buddhism and Advaitism that is, at last, worth discussing. It is better to forget about the presumed conflict, because it is simply not true—it has nothing to do with the Truth at all. In the matter of Truth, then, there is no conflict between the true (or essential) culture of Buddhism and the true (or essential) culture of Advaitism.

To speak as if there were an inherent difference that must be straightened out is to perpetuate the myth that there <u>is</u> an <u>Ultimate</u> difference—when, in Truth, there is <u>no</u> Ultimate difference. In the Ultimate sense, there are no inherently different Realities, no inherently different Truths, no inherently different divinities (or "many gods") in the Inherently Divine Reality Itself. There is a lot of ordinary talk about such multiplicity, and all kinds of ordinary people are pointing (through their traditions) toward "something different" that must, potentially, be Realized (or, otherwise, believed)—but their pointers are simply the mummers' costumes they wear in their ego-based striving and seeking. When such ordinary people come to the Truth Itself, they will have out-grown and relinquished all of that.

DEVOTEE: Beloved Lord, scholarship seems to show that the Advaitins at the time of Shankara, including Gaudapada (the Teacher of Shankara's Teacher), were profoundly affected by the formulations of the "Mahayana" scriptures of Buddhism.

AVATAR ADI DA SAMRAJ: This is one of the matters of ordinary controversy and professional scholarly argument. Thus, it is asked: "Did Advaitism come out of Buddhism? Or did it have its own and independent pre-history? To what degree—or in what stages of their history of mutual association—is there an influence from Buddhism on

Advaitism? To what degree—or in what stages of their history of mutual association—is there an influence from Advaitism on Buddhism?"

Advaitism is not just one thing. There are different schools and Teachers, with many variants. There is no end to this ordinary controversy about whether there is an influence coming from Buddhism that is fundamental to Advaitism. There is no final agreement about it—although, by appealing to scriptures that pre-dated Buddhism, and by demonstrating that essential Teachings of an Advaitic kind were in those texts, Shankara undoubtedly was proving that Advaitism was a pure tradition (in and of itself) and not, in any sense, a mere extension of Buddhism. In fact, Shankara appealed to those traditional texts partly in order to defeat (in His own time) the proposition you just raised. The point is still being argued today in a scholarly form—as if the matter has not been resolved yet, or as if it were important to resolve it. It is not important. It <u>Really</u> is not important.

<u>Truth</u> is important. <u>Realization</u> is important. These petty "ordinary" arguments are just mental "TV". They have no Ultimate importance. In some fundamental terms, Buddhism and Advaitism are two separate traditions—and these two traditions, by arguing with one another and coming into contact with one another, have each (and both) influenced one another in various ways over time.

Both Buddhism and Jainism claim a more ancient origin than their presumed historical founders. Gotama Sakyamuni (at the root of Buddhism) and Mahavir (at the root of Jainism) were contemporaries—and, yet, it is said (by the Jain tradition) that there were many previous Jain "Heroes",[4] going back to a timeless origin, just as Buddhist texts speak in cosmic terms of pre-histories of Gotama Sakyamuni and of many earlier "Buddhas".[5]

In some way, then, the Buddhist and Jain traditions are trying to assert—as a propagandistic argument—that they, like Hinduism, have an ancient origin. Nevertheless, the Buddhist and Jain traditions are each, historically, only approximately twenty-five hundred years old—yet, there are, in fact, Vedic and (according to scholarly estimates) some earliest Upanishadic texts that are considerably older than twenty-five hundred years, and there were Sages and Teachers in the Vedic tradition for a long time before those texts were recorded in written form. In fact, there were many other kinds of traditional (pre-Buddhist and pre-Jain) Teachers who were met by Gotama Sakyamuni and Mahavir. Gotama Sakyamuni and Mahavir did not, themselves, appear out of the blue, such that nobody had ever heard any Transcendental Reality-Teaching before.

No, Gotama Sakyamuni and Mahavir appeared within a circumstance of various pre-existing traditions, with many different schools and Teachers. However, Buddhism and Jainism can assert a similar pre-history to that which is evident in Hinduism only by speaking in poetically expansive terms about previous specifically Buddhist or Jain Realizers, whereas there is no historical evidence for them as such.

Was there a "Mahayana" influence on Advaitism? Certainly Shankara was countering Teachings from the tradition of Buddhism, generating modes of His own argument in order to counter previous arguments of Buddhists. He was not merely sitting in a room writing books, either. According to tradition, He traveled widely and, as was commonplace in those days, visited various royal courts and regional temples, where He entered into debate with other Teachers whom He encountered (who themselves traveled and argued in their various venues). Such philosophical argument was part of the courtly and otherwise sacred "sport" of the time, and many people (of all kinds) among the general public came to listen to these arguments. Therefore, Teachers from all schools "mixed" together, in various circumstances, in their time—arguing with one another in formal debates, and influencing one another in various ways (and not merely in "literary" exchanges). Also, all the while, even though the common people might not themselves have understood much of what exactly the Teachers were saying, they would have a festival while the debates were happening—with much feasting, dancing, and drumming. History and culture are a "mix" of everybody, whereas the ideas proposed in all their literatures may seem (falsely) to have an independent life of their own. In fact, that presumed "independence" (or self-existing separateness) is only a reflection of the ego-mind in the people who read and discuss the ideas presented in the literature of humankind.

In any case, it would seem that Shankara surely did prove the point that there were texts pre-dating all of Buddhism to which He could appeal, by pointing out the Teachings in those texts that correspond to the Advaitic Truth. Those Vedic and earliest Upanishadic texts did not come from Buddhism. On the other hand, Buddhism is not merely in opposition to those Teachings. While arguing on a different basis—not that of scriptural declarations and such, but of simply observing the conditions of life—the same essential Truth was communicated by Gotama Sakyamuni, and, thereafter, in the various traditions of Buddhism.

There is no inherent difference between the essential Truth that was communicated by Gotama Sakyamuni (and other Buddhists) and the essential Truth that was communicated by Shankara (and other Advaitins). The apparent difference that existed was only there at court, between official "Hinduism" (the institutionalized culture that was already in place) and heterodox "Buddhism" (the culture that was encroaching, as a kind of "outsider"). Relative cultural "position" is the source of the conflict.

Fundamentally, Advaitism does not come from Buddhism. That should be obvious, because there are texts containing Advaitic Reality-Teachings that are older than Buddhism. Yet, Advaitism is not Ultimately different from Buddhism. In fact, to non-Hindus, probably among the least interesting things about Shankara is His appeal to traditional scriptural authority—which He does massively, of course, in His great commentaries on the Upanishads, the *Bhagavad Gita,* and the *Brahma Sutras.* He is constantly citing the <u>inherent</u> authority of the traditional scriptural authorities of Hinduism as the guarantor of the Truth of Truths—as if the "conviction" to be Realized comes from the fact that Truth is declared in the scriptures. Therefore, it is (in that view) presumed that scripture is inherently authoritative, and that one need only (in the view of some, at least) sit down and think "I am That"—and, the next thing you know, you <u>are</u> That! Thus, you <u>are</u> That not because you were required to make any profound observations about the Nature of either life (itself) or Reality (Itself), but because the Truth was stated in an official formulation of words that was found in the scriptures—and that is, therefore, as inherently authoritative as if the Divine Spoke It in your ear. However, this must be regarded (especially by non-Hindus) to be among the less persuasive (or rather limited, and non-universal) arguments of traditional Advaitism.

There are, nevertheless, some persuasions within the historical schools of Advaitism that Realization comes about merely through listening to the "Great Declarations" that are found in the traditional scriptures, and that listening to those Declarations alone is <u>sufficient</u> for Realization. Such listening is an exercise that is intensively promoted and practiced by various of the traditional Advaitic schools—but, on the other hand, it is typically required that such practice be carried out only by those who have successfully done much preliminary practicing. Therefore, it is not sufficient to just think "Tat Tvam Asi", "Aham Brahmasmi",[6] and so forth. One must have a foundation. One must arrive with the characteristics that cause the Sage to take you seriously, seriously enough to whisper "Tat Tvam Asi" in your ear, and discipline you, and bring you (by whatever means that particular Sage has) to Realization.

There is no "method" of Realization, based simply on the presumed authority of scripture and the practice of listening to its key statements, that appears in the original scriptural texts otherwise cited by Shankara (or any others). Those Teachings (attributed to Shankara) in which Shankara proposes the earlier scriptures as being both inherently authoritative and the source of the key statements relative to which the practice of listening to the "Great Declarations" is proposed are, in fact, the Teachings originated by Shankara Himself—and, it seems, those particular Teachings were, primarily, originated by Shankara as a defense of Hinduism against "heterodox" opponents, especially

Buddhist opponents. Also, even in the case of Shankara (and others in His Advaita Vedanta school of Advaitism), the "method" of Realization based simply on the presumed authority of scripture and the practice of listening to its key statements does not appear on its own (or as an entirely exclusive practice). Within the tradition of Advaita Vedanta, that "method" was simply a kind of culturally final step, after many presumed preliminaries—preliminaries that were simply presumed (and not necessarily clearly outlined) in the Advaitic texts of Shankara (and others), because there was the prior presumption of the totality of Hindu culture, which served as a vast preliminary and preparatory "school" of discipline, of obligations, and of testing. To be taken seriously by a traditional Advaitic Sage in the Advaita Vedanta school originated by Shankara, you must have successfully gone through (or matured in) that "Hindu school". The traditional Sage did not have to manage that preparatory "school", because the entire culture was "managing" it (so to speak), and the Sage only needed to confirm your therein and thereby "schooled" characteristics of relative maturity.

The traditional Advaitic texts list the characteristics that are necessary to qualify someone to receive Advaitic instruction—and they are the characteristics of the maturity (or preparedness) that come about because the person went to "Hindu school", had been through the process of the culture, and had engaged in various practices (including Yogic practices) and fulfilled various traditionally prescribed duties (including forms of ritually-enacted worship of traditionally prescribed deity-forms). Therefore, that entire "school" of Hinduism and its "root"-authorities—the ancient scriptures—was presumed as a <u>necessary</u> preliminary by traditional Advaita Vedanta.

Buddhism, on the other hand, did not presume any of that. Buddhism was based on a kind of exercise "out in the wilderness". It was part of an ascetical tradition, rather than a tradition that could be lived in the "downtown world" of the larger culture. Therefore, Buddhism originated without appeal to scriptures, without appeal to either traditional authorities or the temple culture. It was an attempt to originate—essentially on the basis of ascetical means—an approach to that same Ultimate Truth that was otherwise the Advaitic essence of the traditional authority of what is now called "Hinduism". The stated purpose of the original Buddhist "procedure" was the transcending of conditionally apparent suffering, rather than the achievement of an otherwise metaphysically described goal. Nevertheless, the Ultimate "result" of that procedure was described as "Nirvana"—otherwise described as the Non-conditional State of the "Unborn".

Similarly, the Jain tradition, which also originated "out in the wilderness", was a tradition that was based on the ascetical life. Thus, originally it was lived apart from the pre-existing national "downtown" culture. Of course, over time, both Jainism and Buddhism became (in their own circumstances of time and place) more and more integrated into the same kind of larger (and not necessarily ascetical) "world" as the general culture with which Advaitism was already associated—a total "world" of all the modes of human living, and duties, and practices, and institutions, temples, and all the rest of it.

At the time of Gotama Sakyamuni, Buddhism was simply a culture of asceticism "out in the wilderness". Over the centuries, Buddhism, like Hinduism, became associated with entire national cultures (especially throughout Asia, but, in the course of time, mostly outside of India)—always including scriptures (of a Buddhist variety), temples, institutions, and a full range of types of practitioners (associated with every kind of mode and stage of life and living). Eventually, Buddhism and Jainism achieved a status that is culturally similar to Hinduism, in that they became part of a complex social enterprise and, thus, incorporated into themselves "universalizing" (or generally inclusive) elements that were not specifically present in their beginnings.

Even though Advaitism declares the authority of its Truth to be present in its scriptures, those who were originally associated with it were living largely in the sphere of asceticism—just as (originally) were Buddhists and Jain practitioners. Therefore, the Advaitism of Shankara is (originally) essentially a practice for sannyasins, just as Buddhism and

Jainism were the equivalent of sannyasin practice (or formal renunciate practice, and ascetical practice), for those few who were of such a
disposition. Nevertheless, all three of these traditions, at least eventually, became integrated with the common "world", the entire "world",
the entire culture. The entire "world", or at least the "world" of their
specific cultural sphere, became the general "school" within which each
tradition was operating and speaking—and, as a result, they each pro-
gressively achieved a very different perspective over time.

The Buddhism of Tibet, for instance, was fully integrated with
the society of Tibet, such that (until recent times) a personage like the
Dalai Lama had not only the authority of a high monk but he was,
effectively, the king of the country—a political figure, as well as what
could be called an ascetic (or at least a professionally renunciate) "religious" figure. In such figures (or professional roles) as the Dalai Lama,
the political and the "religious" were indivisibly blended together.

As "the Buddha", Gotama Sakyamuni was not, in any sense, a political figure. However, according to tradition, He was a political figure
by birth. He was a prince—and, as such, He was fully integrated with
the royal and general culture. However, in His coming to adulthood
(and an accompanying stark familiarity with the sufferings inherent in
the human life-cycle), He renounced His royal position and became an
ascetic, and, eventually, a "Buddha", by dissociating from the royal and,
otherwise, general culture of His birth. By contrast, a Dalai Lama is like
a Gotama Sakyamuni who, eventually, went back home, re-entered the
palace, and re-embraced the culture that, earlier, he had left in order to
follow his quest. The Buddhist and Jain traditions are similar to one
another (and to the Advaitic tradition of Shankara), in that they are
both originally associated with purely ascetical movements, but, ultimately, Buddhism and Jainism each returned to their "home culture",
so to speak, and became integrated with the larger, all-embracing cultural orientation and "school" of life—whereas the Advaitic tradition of
Shankara, while also (originally) being associated with asceticism, never
left its "home" of Hinduism.

Buddhism and Hinduism, generally speaking, are concentrated in different countries. There are Buddhists in India, of course, but, generally, Buddhism is widespread in particular countries where it is identified with other national cultures.

Jainism is peculiar, because it is essentially Indian and never was able to displace Hinduism. Therefore, it has always remained a kind of sub-sect in the "world" of Hinduism—and, generally, one could say, it does not have the kind of global presence that Buddhism has, because Buddhism achieved an identification with cultures outside of India.

3.

DEVOTEE: Beloved, You Say that no rational speech, and no irrational speech, but only the language of ecstasy can speak Realization. You Say:

> *Can you see why even right Instruction is Paradox? Reasonable and irrational descriptions—without paradoxes, and without the Ultimate Paradox of Eternal Unity and Eternal Relationship—are, necessarily, only for those who are ego-possessed and who refuse to practice the Way.*[7]

It has always seemed to me that one of the aspects of Your Unique Reality-Teaching is Your emphasis on "limitless relatedness" as not different from Consciousness.

It seems that there is a Great Paradox that has never been fully articulated or embraced in its completeness, in the history of the Great Tradition.

AVATAR ADI DA SAMRAJ: The paradoxes are matters of "point of view", or modes of speech associated with the developmental stages of life. If I Speak in Address to a person who is of the disposition of maturity represented by the first three stages of life, or, otherwise, the fourth stage of life, or the fifth stage of life, or the sixth stage of life, what I Say Speaks to that disposition, and Critically Addresses its egoic characteristics. What I would Say to any other in a different disposition—or in a mode of maturity that is characterized by a particular stage of life otherwise—would seem to be different, even contradictory, when compared to what I have perhaps Stated to another, in a different disposition (or stage of life). If you would happen to hear the Statements made by Me to different individuals, you might ask, "You Said such and such to Humpty, and such and such to Dumpty. And these separate 'Humpty' and 'Dumpty' doctrines completely contradict one another."

And then I Say, "Well—you see what a Paradox My Teaching Really Is."

The apparent paradox that is associated with the comparisons between the different stages of life is not, ultimately, a paradox (or some kind of irreducibly self-contradictory dilemma) at all. It is Self-Evident, and there is no inherent essential "difference" in it, and no problem, no contradiction, no dilemma, and nothing that needs to be explained. Therefore, the seventh stage Realization and Its Characteristics are not, ultimately, paradoxical. It is simply that, when it comes time to Speak to people based on their stage of maturity and necessities of practice, the prism cuts the light in different colors—six times.

Is the existence of red <u>and</u> blue a paradox? In some sense, can it be said that the apparent difference between the fifth stage disposition and the disposition of the sixth stage of life is a paradox? Is the apparent difference between the sixth stage disposition and the third stage disposition a paradox? It is the same as asking if two different colors, because they both exist, are a kind of illogical paradox in Reality—when, in fact, there is no inherent essential difference at all. The Divine Conscious Light is Colorless—All-White, only "Bright". There is no distinction in It. And, yet, everything arises and is comprehended in It.

When "Humpty-Dumpty" is not yet fallen and broken—"Humpty" and "Dumpty" are one. When "Humpty-Dumpty" is fallen and broken, the one appears to be not only many but, also, a fragmentation of what was one. Nevertheless, the lament of the "point of view" that sees Reality as separate conditions is that Reality cannot be "put together again".

In Most Perfect Realization, there are no ultimate paradoxes, because there are no comparisons to be made. However, in the sphere of the developmental stages of life—and, thus, in the sphere of minds, or in the sphere of mummery, or in the sphere of egos—there are apparent differences everywhere. Thus, when Utterances are made that correspond to the exactnesses of the apparent differences, those Utterances (when compared to one another) seem paradoxical—and, perhaps, irreconcilable.

In terms of "limitless relatedness", and its being a matter insisted upon by Me in My Teaching overall—that term is always a mode of My Speaking of Non-"difference", of no dissociation into "otherness", or into apparent relatedness through separation. The "method" of dissociation is the "method" of egoity. The "method" of superimposing "difference"—of superimposing separateness, separation, separativeness, and dissociation altogether—is the "method" of egoity and the characteristic of egoity. The feeling of relatedness is the "root"-characteristic of egoity itself. Paradoxically (or so it seems), the feeling of relatedness contains within itself the feeling of separateness, of otherness, and of "difference"—whereas, if you simply speak the word "relatedness", it does not immediately sound as if there is any "difference"-making suggested there. Somehow the word "relatedness" suggests some kind of union (or unity)—but, in Truth, it does not.

The feeling of relatedness is founded on the feeling of separateness, and it defines that to which it is related as "other", or "object". The feeling of relatedness is inherently associated with presumed differences, not with Non-"difference". The feeling of relatedness is an invention of egoity. There is no "difference". There is only the Indivisible Reality, Which Always Already has the Characteristic of Indivisibility. How, then, can there be any inherent differences? There are none.

There are none. It is not that there are differences and they must be overcome. There <u>are</u> no differences. Why does it <u>seem</u> that there <u>are</u> differences, then?

You are, at this moment, "experiencing" the sense of separate "self", and of "others", and of "objects", and of "difference", and of relatedness—right now. It is not <u>enough</u> for Me to simply <u>Say</u> that "difference" does not exist. I <u>am</u> Saying it: It does not exist! There is <u>no</u> "difference". There <u>is</u> no "difference". Yet, you <u>are</u> declaring "difference"—you <u>are</u> "experiencing" it, now. Indeed, you are (and have been) building an entire lifetime on "difference". You are counting on its being the case for every breath. And, therefore, you are making a life based on this very presumption (of inherent "difference") that, in Truth, has no Real (or inherent) existence whatsoever.

The feeling of relatedness is not Real. It is not so. When you Realize that it is not so—then, it <u>is</u> <u>not</u> so. Until you Realize that it is not so, it <u>is</u> so. When I am Speaking to someone for whom "difference", and otherness, and relatedness, and separateness are seemingly self-evident reality, it does not seem worth My spending too much time Saying, "None of that is existing." Some kind of process must be endured, if it is no longer to be the case that you are suffering this illusion of separateness, relatedness, otherness, and "difference". That process is all the foundation practices of the Reality-Way of Adidam—and the Reality-Way of Adidam is (in Its totality) the total process of your devotional (and, thus and thereby, ego-transcending) relationship to Me.

Your devotional relationship to Me does require Me to, in the Instructional manner, be conformed to your sense of inherent "difference", your bondage, your separateness, your questions, your states of mind, your illusions. I must Function here with you, while you are living and existing in a totally "self"-deluded state—a state, that, to Me, is self-evidently not the case. Therefore, I Speak to you in terms that relate to all the apparently different modes of your "experiencing".

The modes of conditional "experiencing" are virtually infinite—but they are also definable, in very limited terms, relative to the structures of the body-mind-complex and the stages of life. Thus, I can Speak to you, over time, in varying modes of language, each of which is Instructive and useful to you in the particular moment. And, in fact, among the texts in this book, there appears the following:

I. The Orientation of Practice Based Upon the "Disposition" of Identification With the Body:

"Based upon the 'disposition' of identification with the body, I am the devotee-servant of the bodily apparent Person of my inherently perfect Guru—the true Master-Sage to whom my body and mind are constantly surrendered."

II. The Orientation of Practice Based Upon the "Disposition" of Identification With the Mind:

"Based upon the 'disposition' of identification with the mind, I am like an idea, yielding toward devotional unity (or re-union) with the infinite Spiritual matrix (or ascended Bliss-Mind) of my inherently perfect Guru—the true Master-Sage to whom my body and mind are constantly surrendered."

III. The Orientation of Practice Based Upon the "Disposition" of the Intrinsically Self-Evident Self-Condition That Is Consciousness Itself:

"Based upon the 'Disposition' of Intrinsic Self-Identification with Consciousness itself, I am not separated from the Self-existing and Self-radiant State of my perfectly Self-Realized Guru. Therefore, by means of the ego-surrendering exercise of non-difference, my devotion is perfectly maintained, and I need only Self-Abide in the ultimate knowledge of the Heart-Current of Bliss, in which I am constantly Blessed to be Awake by the Compassionate Regard of my inherently perfect Guru—the true Master-Sage to whom my body and mind are constantly surrendered."[8]

In My Rendering of this traditional text, three different kinds of statements are made—one from the "disposition" of egoic "self"-identification with the body, another from the "disposition" of egoic "self"-identification with the mind, and the third from the "Disposition" of Intrinsic Self-Identification with the Transcendental Self-Condition. Thus, each statement speaks in a different mode. Each statement speaks truly, authentically—but on a specific "identity"-basis that is (in each case) different from the statement made from each of the other "dispositions" (or bases of "identity" and understanding). What is said authentically on each such basis, in the true devotional manner in which each statement (or "confession") is spoken, is true speech—although, paradoxically, it is a different kind of speech than is made from either of the other two positions.

Therefore, there are necessary apparent paradoxes of speech, apparent paradoxes of "knowledge", apparent paradoxes even in the life of devotion to the one and only Master of your life. It is simply that your degree of maturity determines the characteristics of your devotion. Nevertheless, the characteristics demonstrated on the basis of any one of the "Three Dispositions" of practice are authentic in the case of every devotee who (thus) practices rightly—regardless of his or her stage of maturity.

Your "disposition" today, it is hoped, is perhaps more mature (and somehow different) from what it might have been ten or twenty years ago in My Divine Avataric Company. Thus, you can point to a kind of apparent paradox in the comparison between your "disposition" of years ago and your "disposition" of today. At each stage of maturity, the understanding (although it may be authentic) is apparently different than the understanding expressed at the other stages.

The orientations associated with the six developmental stages of life are the potential seeking-"dispositions" of every human being—unless the practice truly and consistently becomes the "radical" (or always "at-the-root") seventh stage Reality-Way of only-by-Me Revealed and Given Adidam (Which inherently transcends all possible modes of seeking and all merely conditionally-based and ego-based "dispositions" and modes of practice). Otherwise, in any and every case, the characteristics of the "disposition" at each of the six developmental stages of life are inevitable—and each of the six developmental stages of life is governed by the conditional and ego-based structures of the body-mind-"self". What I might Say to someone in his or her integrity as a devotee of Mine at his or her present stage of development would presumably be different (in some respects) than at another point in that same individual's development.

Have I Addressed your actual question?

DEVOTEE: You have Answered it absolutely and completely, Beloved.

AVATAR ADI DA SAMRAJ: Tcha.[9]

4.

DEVOTEE: Beloved Lord, I was once a Buddhist before I came to Your Feet—a practitioner of Rinzai Zen Buddhism, including koan study and meditation. One thing that is wonderfully profound about Your Offering to humankind is that the person immediately finds out that there is this activity called "Narcissus", and that one's suffering has everything to do with one's own activity. Nobody ever mentioned that to me, even though I had an authentic Buddhist teacher.

Is this understanding something that Buddhism just does not emphasize? Does Buddhism understand that we have this activity of egoic "self"-identification? Or is it really not understood at all?

AVATAR ADI DA SAMRAJ: About whom are you asking? Are you asking it about someone in particular? Or about a tradition in general?

How can there be a tradition in general? That is nobody. How can you attribute any particularity of understanding to a tradition as a whole—when every kind of understanding, lack of understanding, and misunderstanding can be found in the totality of everyone associated with that tradition?

My Divine Avataric Reality-Teaching to you about the matter of most fundamental "self"-understanding is a Unique Teaching—a "Radical" Teaching, an "At-the-Root" Teaching, at the "root" of what egoity really is. This Divine Avataric Reality-Teaching is not found in the traditions. Its preciseness is not there. However, there are modes of understanding here and there that are shown, demonstrated, uttered, written, in various of the traditions, which obviously reflect upon the matter of bondage, or egoity, and the transcending of it.

Therefore, there is a stream of such understanding to be found in the traditions of Buddhism—yet, that understanding is not identical to My Divine Avataric Reality-Teaching. It is not simply that you can find My Unique Reality-Teaching there. You can find some elements of It there—but only My Own Teaching-Revelation is altogether Complete and "At-the-Root".

However, as I Said, one cannot (except in an only metaphorical or poetic sense) rightly speak about a tradition as if it were a person. On the one hand, such a generalization may have metaphorical value, for the sake of conversation—in order to allow for something or other to be spoken about. Yet, on the other hand, it is also a wrong idea. There is no tradition that is a person. There have been millions of Buddhists— people thinking and living in terms of Buddhist terminology, Buddhist language, Buddhist philosophy, Buddhist practice—and there are many different modes of Buddhist practice. Very immature people have been associated with Buddhism, as well as people of profundity and people of great Realization.

Therefore, what is the tradition? Who is that? A tradition is not a person. Buddhism is not a person.

There is, traditionally, some attempt to make Gotama Sakyamuni "the person" (or "the Buddha") of Buddhism, and to attribute to Him all of the ideas, all of the doctrines, all of the Teachings found in all this vast communication made by Buddhists for the last twenty-five hundred years. This is an example of fictional attribution, whereby an historical culture (perhaps originated by a true Realizer, but otherwise developed and changed by others over time) is represented (and even personified) by a person of significance, but to the extreme degree, of being identified as that person—even a supposed historical person (such as Gotama Sakyamuni). Nevertheless, all of that is, at last, only the nonsense of the mumming mind of egoity.

If there were the equivalent, in the tradition of Buddhism, of My Divine Avataric Reality-Teaching—in all of its parts and in summary— I would tell you. However, there is no equivalent anywhere in the Great Tradition of humankind. Yet, it is not simply that I am Saying so. Examine it yourself. This by-Me-Given and by-Me-Demonstrated Revelation is All-Completing and Unique. That does not mean that It has nothing to do with what came before. It is Continuous with what came before, and It Completes what came before, and It Criticizes aspects of what came before. Yet, there is no equivalent of My Divine Avataric Reality-Teaching in the Great Tradition, nor is My Divine Avataric Reality-Teaching to be found in the unified totality of the Great Tradition.

The Great Tradition is not "anyone". The Great Tradition is not even "everyone". The Great Tradition is words. Who is words? Nobody. The language is speaking for itself. It is, in the "world" of today, as if everyone is meditating on the language and trying to find some kind of secret in the grammar that will Illuminate their minds—as if the language itself has the hidden secret, and one need only elaborate the inherent capability of language in order to arrive at "absolute knowledge", or "everything-knowledge". Such is part of the mythology of a culture and a time that is obsessed with acquiring power over things by means of the exercise of "knowing" things.

There is a seeming paradox in Reality—such that Realization of Reality (Itself) has nothing to do with "knowledge". When I use the term "Perfect (or Ultimate) Knowledge", I mean something not at all like conventional (or conditional) "knowledge". When I use a term such as "Perfect Knowledge", I am Speaking about Transcendental Realization. Nevertheless, "Perfect Knowledge" (or Transcendental Realization) has nothing whatsoever to do with the mind. And, yet, if you were to try to suppress the mind, so as to achieve That in Which there is no mind, you would never find It. So, that is not it, either.

The mind is a vehicle of seeking. It just goes on and on and on.

You say you were a Buddhist. However, I did not have to become an institutional Buddhist, or an exclusive Buddhist advocate, in order to Speak the "Buddhist Truth".

In any case, Truth Itself has nothing to do with having such an identity. I am not a "Buddhist", or a "Hindu", or anything else of the kind. Sheerly as a matter of conversation, or to speak in one or another manner in order to explain and elaborate, words are used, utterances are made. You all have listened to Me Speak now for several hours. And, earlier, I read traditional texts to you as well. What do you remember of any of it? How much do you remember? What do you remember? What have you remembered? If you are remembering anything of it, what you are remembering is some selection, some angle on what has been Spoken, that has to do with your train of mind, your habit of thinking, your disposition in the moment, your limitations of egoity in the moment. In any case, your memory is not about Realization.

Therefore, true Realization requires ego-transcending devotional surrender and Ultimate Grace. You must grow beyond (by out-growing your limitations) in My Divine Avataric Company—for Real, by Means of devotional turning to Me. Be Instructed and Awakened by Great Means, Transcendental Spiritual Means, in My Divine Avataric Company. The Real process is that wherein Realization is made Real. Everything else is talk.

I have viewed the Making of this book—and, also, the Making of the larger book, *The Gnosticon,* from which this book has been drawn— to be worth doing. *The Gnosticon* has potential use for people—and, so, I have Made It. Nevertheless, neither this book nor *The Gnosticon* as a whole is sufficient, in and of itself, to bring people to Realization. It may bring them to <u>Me</u>—and, then, the process can begin, if you stay turned to Me.

The Real process is not about having a conversation with Me. I am always making sure that I have Said what needs to be Said, and Provided you with the Means of Instruction that are necessary—but the relationship to Me that is the Real process of Realization is not a conversation. Conversation is merely incidental, or ordinary. All there is of Realization, all there is of Reality Itself and Truth Itself, is Self-Manifested before you, right now—<u>As</u> Me. That Being the Case for each of you here, now, in this room with Me—what are you Realizing?

It is enough to come into My Divine Avataric Company—but, if (as is inevitable, in the general case) Realization is not Perfected here, in this instant, then the relationship to Me must continue (in the terms that are necessary for your growth and out-growing), such that (by all My Means) Realization is Awakened for Real in your case.

In all the years of My Divine Avataric Teaching-Work and My Divine Avataric Revelation-Work, I have Communicated the "Perfect Practice" of the only-by-Me Revealed and Given Reality-Way of Adidam— Showing It to you in My Own Person and Speaking It to you variously. Yet, the conversation My devotees have required has always (characteristically) been of a lesser nature—associated with the characteristics of egoity in which you are bound, and the habits of mind and life by which you are patterned. Therefore, all of that has been Addressed by Me. Nevertheless, My "Perfect Practice" Teaching is My Ultimate and Essential Word to you. Whatever I Must Animate or Speak to you in order to Bring you to the point of availability for this "Perfect Practice" and Realization is all of the rest that I Do—other than to simply Be here.

Questions can have use, if they are asked from that position in which you are absolutely vulnerable and in absolute need of Instruction. If you were asking Me such a true question, you would be physically very uncomfortable and sweating. You would be in humanly real trouble.

Or, let Me put it this way: You <u>are</u> in humanly real trouble—and, in the case of your true question, you would truly <u>know</u> that you are in humanly real trouble.

In general, however, you do not know that you are in humanly real trouble. You do not get it. You are distracted, preoccupied, ego-possessed, moving by desire, seeking. You do not truly notice and inspect what is happening. You do not notice the situation you are, humanly, really in—not conditionally, and not Ultimately.

My Divine Avataric Transcendental Spiritual Work has always been profoundly Urgent—because I Know what is actually happening with every one. You would do well to become profoundly serious. If you could become profoundly serious, by comprehending the <u>inherent</u> trouble of humankind—and not merely the present-time "daily news" kind of trouble—the matter of Realization would be close by. It would be your absolute need, the only possible satisfaction.

In fact, it is to such a "troubled" one that these traditional texts are Spoken (now, by Me). Effectively, it is to such a one that I am always Speaking—even though, in fact, human beings are distracted, bound in their own thinking and desiring. Yet, what I am Speaking to you in My "Perfect Practice" Teaching is an Utterance made in Absolute Urgency to any one and every one who is in greatest need—and, thus, to all who can see the actual situation. If you cannot see it yet, then there is much growth and out-growing, and, altogether, much "self"-discipline, in which you will (necessarily) have to participate, in order to come even to that point of true need. Indeed, it is only when you have come to the point of Perfect Urgency that it is possible for you to Realize the Perfect Truth Itself.

As long as there is <u>anything</u> at all that can divert you, for now, distract you, for now, occupy you, for now, or be enough for you, for now—you cannot rightly and fully comprehend the situation that you are in, and you do not (and cannot yet) "Perfectly Know" the Transcendental Nature of Reality (Itself). The authors of the traditional texts that I have Rendered into English in this book were individuals Who knew the humanly real trouble, and Who had, Themselves, become Urgent—and profoundly serious. Their seriousness made Their Awakening necessary—and Their seriousness made Them available to the Awakeners Who would make Their Awakening Really possible, and, at last, Really So.

Therefore, your whatever degree of seriousness is bringing you to Me now, and that is the basis for the "Bond" you make with Me—wherein the relationship to Me can work for the Sake of your Awakening. And I am always here to Magnify that seriousness, and that (potential) Perfect Urgency, in you.

There is the terrible mass of threats associated with this "late-time" (or "dark" epoch)—but it is also a fact that you do not have much time in any case (or in any time or epoch). Life is short, and, because of egoity, it is bewildered and wandering. Because of egoity, it is anxious and afraid. None of that is necessary. The transcending of egoity is possible—Awakening is possible—because of the Nature of Reality Itself.

In order to become profoundly serious, you must become disillusioned with your egoic patterning. You must become inherently (and not merely negatively) disillusioned with every thing and every one. Such disillusionment is not despair. Rather, it is clarity—and it is inevitably associated with a magnification of sympathy, not with dissociation.

The "world" is ego-mummery. The "world" is mad. Humankind is in a constant state of extreme psychosis—don't you know? Therefore, knowing that, choose to take the cure.

Various kinds of advice are given in the traditional texts that I have presented to you in this book. Those modes of advice, generally speaking, are associated with certain limitations. As such, they are what you could call "preliminary instructions". Yet, apart from those limited aspects of these traditional texts, the fundamental Voice and the fundamental Teaching in them is a Teaching that I am Speaking to you.

In *The Gnosticon*, I present a principal "Perfect Practice" Text that is simply My Own Divine Avataric Reality-Teaching—without any association with traditional texts. Therefore, in *The Gnosticon,* you may read My Perfect Utterance that Clarifies all matters greatly and further. I have put *Eleutherios* in *The Gnosticon,*[10] with all these traditional texts (which are outstanding within the Great Tradition)—and I have Spoken even the traditional texts Myself, by Standing beyond all the cultures of "difference", and by Standing with (and As) the Realization-Voice at the heart of each text, such that the texts are, each and all, Spoken in and by Means of My Own and Single Voice.

This Reality-Teaching I Speak is True—Perfectly True.

This Reality-Teaching I Speak is not merely a matter of report. I Confirm It to you.

This Reality-Teaching I Speak Is the Only Truth.

This Reality-Teaching I Speak Is Reality Itself—and Reality Itself Is Truth Itself, and the Only Real (Acausal) God.

This Reality-Teaching I Speak is not merely the conditional reality of your mumming, but It Is Reality Itself—That Which can and must be Realized, That Which Transcends all, That Which Is Perfectly Sufficient, even while this arising seems, because It Is the Nature of even all of this, but not from any "point of view".

5.

AVATAR ADI DA SAMRAJ: There Is a Non-conditional Condition to be Realized, Which Is Non-separate and Utterly without "point of view"—and That Non-conditional Condition Is the True Self-Nature, Self-Condition, and Self-State of all-and-All. Gotama Sakyamuni was moved to speak of the Realization of That Truth in terms of a disposition that wanted to escape. That was His metaphor of need. That is how His seriousness was characterized. His participation in life was so unarmored that He had absolutely no tolerance for conditional existence whatsoever. It was, to Him, only suffering, darkness, madness, and bewilderment—and His entire disposition was motivated to escape it. That motivation gave Him the energy for His course of discipline and Awakening.

One's seriousness might be characterized in other ways—yet, nevertheless, true Reality-Awakening is entirely about the transcending of egoity. Perfect Realization is about the transcending of egoity. Truth Itself, Reality Itself, is about the Perfect transcending of egoity—not in the "elsewhere", but in That Which <u>Is</u> Always Already <u>The</u> Case. Since It <u>Is</u> So, and Self-Evidently So, but not <u>apparently</u> So to you—clearly, the necessary course is one of transcending your own limitation, your own egoity, your own imposition on Reality Itself. That course is necessary because, if it were not for your own imposition, That Which <u>Is</u> Always Already <u>The</u> Case would be Self-Evident in your own case— because It <u>Is</u> <u>Always</u> <u>Already</u> <u>The</u> <u>Case</u>.

That Which is to be Realized is not "somewhere else". It is not a "something else". It is not a "someone else". It <u>Is</u> Always Already <u>The</u> Case. It <u>Is</u> <u>The</u> One and Only Case. However, It is not, for now, Always Already Self-Evident to you. Therefore, <u>you</u> are your problem.

I am Enabling you to transcend yourself, by Giving you Means and Blessing for the transcending of egoity. That is, essentially, My Divine Avataric Word to you. Such is what there is to be serious about, what there is to do, and what there is to make the focus of your life. That is the discipline. That is the Way I have Given to you.

Rather than watch you all suffer to death, I would rather that you Awaken now. My Urgency is to Break Through your barriers here— your obstructions, your resistance, your "self"-contraction—to Enable you to Realize My Inherently Perfect (Intrinsically egoless, and Non-conditional) Self-Nature, Self-Condition, and Self-State. <u>Now</u>. If you Realize Me Most Perfectly, all of the inevitable struggle and suffering and extraordinary horror of conditionally manifested existence is <u>Utterly</u> Outshined in My Love-Bliss-"Brightness".

The Divine Freedom of Reality Itself is Free of all struggle and suffering—even in the face of struggle and suffering. That Which is to be Realized is not merely "behind the eyes", nor merely "inside". It is not dissociated. It is not based on any such device or "method". What must be Self-Realized <u>As</u> Consciousness (<u>Itself</u>) is, in Truth, the same as "everything in the room". You simply do not yet Divinely Self-Recognize the room itself, and all that is in the room. You are defined by "point of view", by perception in the context of this space-of-others, defined by your own act of "self"-contraction.

Therefore, I Call That Which is to be Realized by other Names—such as "the 'Bright'", and the "Conscious Light"—intending, by these terms, to make it clear to you that Realization is not about any exclusionary fastening upon inwardness.

The Most Perfect Divine Self-Realization of Which I Speak does not depend upon any conditional state that is associated with any particular arrangement of the body-mind-complex. My Perfect (Non-conditional, egoless, and Acausal) Divine Self-Realization Is Beyond all psycho-physical conditions—and, therefore, Beyond all psycho-physically based forms of Spiritual effort.

When That Which Is Self-Existing and Self-Radiant Consciousness Itself (or the Divine Conscious Light) is Most Perfectly Realized, the "world" is (Inherently) Divinely Self-Recognized. Everything otherwise apparently "other" or "different" is Divinely Self-Recognized As That—not by some operation of mind, and not merely by participation in some kind of metaphor, or by using any kind of conditionally applied device at all. Rather, Divine Self-Recognition of all-and-All Is Self-Evidently So. There is no "difference". There is no "other". There is no "separate self". There is only Real God, the God Who Is Reality Itself—the Non-conditional, Acausal, Transcendental, Self-Existing, Self-Radiant Reality (Itself)—and not the myths of mind, the myths of culture, or the institutionalized myths of the "world"-mummery.

There is not an "other" consciousness. There are no "others" in the room. There is no "thing". I Say So—and these traditional texts Say So. They testify likewise. It is the Truth, and It can be Realized. The Means for the Most Perfect Realization of That Truth is here Present, As Me, for you—Offered to you, in Most Complete Form.

I Am here—now, and forever hereafter.

I Am That.

IX

THE WAY OF KNOWLEDGE THAT BECOMES POSSIBLE ONLY AT THE FINAL STAGE OF MATURITY

The Reality-Teachings of The Advaitic Sage of The Devikalottara

The Devikalottara *is an Upagama, a supplemental text associated with the* Vatulagama, *one of the twenty-eight Sanskrit works in the Saiva Siddhanta tradition written in the period leading up to the turn of the Common Era. These texts form some of the earliest expositions of Saiva religious doctrine and practice, and remain influential today in South Indian Saivism. The* Devikalottara, *also known as* Caturvimsatisahasrakalottara *("the Kalottara in 24,000 verses"), is one of many recensions of the* Kalottara *(or Kalajnana)* Upagama, *which was likely appended to its parent* Vatulagama *text during the first millennium CE. The text is presented in the form of a dialogue between Devi and Siva, and is known in Tamil as well as in Sanskrit.*

The true right devotee (approaching the Sage of the *Devikalottara* with great respect, and humbly, in the traditional devotional manner) says:

1. Master of all! I would surely know the Way and the practice by which true liberation can certainly be achieved, by one and all. Be pleased, in your heart of Grace, to Reveal the true Way and its discipline to me.

The Master-Sage of the *Devikalottara* (in heartfelt response to the respectfully approaching devotee—and with utmost kindness, moved by the fullness of compassionate regard there-evoked by the honest maturity of rightest-made devotion) speaks:

2. Good person, so honorably intent! Yes, for the sake of every one and all, I will now Reveal to you, in fullest and straightforward explanations, the Way of final knowing, and the summary of its necessary discipline. This Way and its practice can be rightly understood only by those of evident maturity in devotional and Spiritual right life. Nevertheless, if such serious persons will embrace the discipline of this ultimate course I will Reveal to you—they will know true liberation, by Realizing That Which <u>Is</u>, utterly prior to all combining with conditionally apparent forms and activities.

3. Most serious and well-spoken one! You must appreciate that anyone of lesser maturity—who is, therefore, at heart, incapable of understanding this Way of final knowing—could not otherwise come to this understanding, even if countless books of explanation were read, and thoughts of "Revelation" were erected all around, as infinite in number as the particles of cosmic space.

4. However, if you, or anyone at all, is already well-founded in devotional and Spiritual right life—then, be given over entirely to this Way of final knowing I will now Reveal to you. Be established in the firmest disposition—free of all anxieties and doubts about this final course. Be renounced of all conditionally arising attachments

and desires—and, with a clarity born of perfect absence of all confused or ambiguous states of mind, be intensely heart-devoted to the Self-Realization of ultimate and final knowing.

5. If you, or anyone at all, would practice the Way of final knowing, you must, first, become equipped with preparatory virtues—made by "self"-discipline and, altogether, right life. Therefore, if and when renunciation of "ownership" (or egoic identification and egoic clinging) relative to all others and things is true of you, and, also, active sympathetic regard of all is your constant demonstration (such that you are the truly "harmless" relation of all), and, ultimately, when the total Yogic discipline of body, mind, and ego-"I" is matured to such degree that you are entirely and one-pointedly focused on liberation-only—then (and only then), you should intensively and constantly study this, my Teaching of the Way of final knowing, and engage its practice steadily, with all your heart's intent, to make its single Realization finally true of you.

6. The mind is much the same as a natural force—like weather and a wind. It moves like water's ever-changing course, and never finally stops by force of any counter-thought or will to otherwise. Nevertheless, only one in whom the mind is truly brought under control is (thus and thereby) prepared to practice the Way of final knowing. The goal of all preparatory practices—whether of right life by exercise of "self"-discipline, or virtue, or Yogic and Spiritual means—is true and complete control of the mind.

7. Indeed, the means to attain true liberation is, itself, the very means whereby the mind is, at last, perfectly controlled. That unique and final means—or Way of final knowing—is the inherently perfect steady-State that is Consciousness itself. Therefore, know this with perfect certainty—beyond all mind of doubts and change.

8. When the mind appears or changes—even to the slightest degree—<u>that</u> is bondage. When the mind neither arises nor follows on itself—<u>that</u> is liberation. This is, clearly, so. Therefore, <u>how</u> is liberation from the mind to be achieved? What is the requirement—or the State—in which the mind neither arises nor follows on itself? It is the State of final knowing—the intrinsically Self-Evident State of Self-Awareness of Consciousness itself. The means of perfect (or intrinsic and permanent) control of the mind is to Self-Abide <u>as</u> the intrinsic State (or mere Self-Awareness) of Consciousness <u>itself</u>.

9. The inherent happiness that is Realized by Self-Abiding merely <u>as</u> the Self-Awareness of Consciousness itself <u>is</u> limitless, ultimate, and perfect Bliss. <u>That</u> Bliss-Consciousness is the inherently actionless Supreme Reality. Tell me, how could any intelligent person not rejoice in this Truth-Revelation of Reality itself?

10. Merely by Self-Abiding <u>as</u> That Which is all-pervading, prior to mind—prior to all "objects", all forms, all others, and all knowledge of the "world"—the any one made <u>thus</u> wise by final knowing attains perfect true liberation, utterly without efforts of seeking.

11. The arising of any "point of view" <u>in</u> space self-manifests an inherent characteristic of association with active differentiated energy, moving out toward (or in and throughout) <u>all</u> space. That energy is what is traditionally called "Shakti" (and, also, "Spirit"). The entire cosmic universe is lighted by that energy—the cosmic shine of Spirit everywhere. The "point of view" (or ego-"I") in space proceeds by thought alone—that modifies the energy of its regard (and its arisings of desire and seeking) in the everywhere of space. Thus, both form and time arise by means of thoughts of ego-"I" in space—and even <u>all</u> the cosmic universe is merely thought's own Spirit-fabrications, made by "self"-contraction to a "point of view"

in space. Therefore, the State that is inherently free of "point of view"—of ego-"I", of thought, of space, of time, of form, of cosmic universe at all, and all the Spirit-motions fabricating universal seeming everywhere—<u>is</u> the final knowing to be Realized.

12. The one and indivisible Self-Consciousness—infinite, formless, all-pervading, non-dual, and Self-radiant—<u>is</u>, itself, the means of perfect true liberation, because it <u>is</u> That Which is to be Realized.

13. The Way of final knowing is the <u>only</u> direct path to liberation—by means of inherent (tacit, or mind-transcending) Self-Abiding <u>as</u> the Self-Evident Reality Which <u>is</u> Consciousness (<u>itself</u>), and Which <u>is</u> Bliss (or the inherently actionless Self-radiance, or intrinsic and inherently perfect Spirit-energy, of Consciousness <u>itself</u>). One who is truly prepared (by every right and necessary preliminary means) to practice this Way of final knowing need not (and should not) any longer meditate on Yogic centers of energy in the body, or on nerve-currents of energy in the body, or on internal subtle sounds and lights, or on programs of internal visualization (of deities and the like), or on programs of secret words of prayerful invocation and internalized worship, or on any magic formulas supposed to recruit cosmic entities for the sake of controlling natural powers, or in order to achieve control over the future.

14. One who is rightly and truly prepared to practice the Way of final knowing, and who is (thus and thereby) given over to the Reality of perfect true liberation, need not (and should not) any longer practice psycho-physically activated (or conditional) Yogic methods of breath-control, concentration, meditation, and contemplative absorption.

15. In the true right practice of the Way of final knowing, there is <u>no</u> exercise of body or mind to be activated for the sake of knowing

anything that can be known outside (or as other than) the Self-Evident State of Consciousness itself and its inherent (or Self-radiant) Self-Condition (of Bliss itself). Therefore, listen to me and hear me: The Way of final knowing is the ancient ultimate Teaching of Truth—and it is entirely and only the Way of Self-Abiding Self-knowledge of Consciousness <u>itself</u>, without any associated knowledge of whatever is <u>not</u>-Self (or not Consciousness, <u>itself</u>).

16. For those whose minds are in perpetual motion in and among and within the space and time and "objects" of their "point of view", there is no end to the arising of conditions of bondage. Therefore, know this: There is <u>no</u> suffering in any kind of world, for one in whom the wandering mind is turned about, upon its Source, and, thereby, vanished in the one and Self-Evident State that is Consciousness itself—always already prior to world, body, mind, and ego-"I" (or "point of view").

17. Merely Self-Abide <u>as</u> That Which <u>is</u> one, indivisible, complete, perfect, and all-pervading—relative to Which there is no "inside", and relative to Which there is no "outside", and relative to Which there is neither "above" nor "below" nor any whatever in between, and of Which every apparently arising form or "object" or "other" is a merely apparent Self-modification, but Which is <u>itself</u> perfectly (or always already) formless. <u>That</u> one and only one is Self-existing and Self-radiant—and it is not knowable by any means (or via any apparent relation or modification of itself), but it can (and must) be Self-Revealed, and thereby known, as and by means of itself alone.

18. People tend to live and act in an egoically patterned manner, with little "self"-understanding, and in casual accordance with their randomly acquired desires and all the accumulated motives of their seeking in this world. The result is the usual destiny, ego-caused,

frustrated by natural conjunctions, and bound tight in a maze of suffering and dead ends. Observing this, do not do likewise. Renounce the life of purposeful bondage. Turn attention away from the theatre of "objects". Be concentrated on the invisible, the non-"objective" Self, the intrinsic Self-Awareness of Consciousness itself.

19. In the native Self-Condition of Consciousness itself, conditional and "objective" phenomena are inherently non-existent and not known. Therefore, in Consciousness itself, actions, causation, effects, theories about "Reality", single anything, multiple anythings, duality, even the world itself, and even individuals living in bondage to the world are all without existence—and, indeed, they are not known at all.

20. The totality of the apparent cosmic universe is nothing but the one and indivisible Self-existing and Self-radiant Reality that is its underlying foundation and only substance. The apparent light of the apparent cosmic universe is a merely-seeming shine—made luminous by the real persistence of the underlying Self-radiance of Self-existing Consciousness itself. The perfect Yogi always turns inward, toward the underlying Reality, rather than outward, toward the apparent cosmic universe. In this manner, even every "object" in the world ceases to be different from its Source. Therefore, know this secret of right practice.

21. Anyone who does not turn within, upon the underlying Reality of Self-existing and Self-radiant Consciousness (itself), is a mere worldling, in constant bondage to the merely-seeming world—like a lowly silkworm, permanently wrapped and enclosed in its self-made capsule of silk. Therefore, understand this lesson about wrong practice.

22. Even all living beings, of every species and kind, merely suffer—repeatedly and terminally. Therefore, listen to my Teaching, and hear it well: If you would be free of all suffering and of all that

merely comes to a terminal end—be <u>constantly</u> turned upon the underlying indivisible Reality of Consciousness <u>itself</u>.

23. The modes of "self"-discipline and of virtue that constitute right life are traditionally prescribed, for <u>all</u> seekers—in order to prepare them for the ultimate practice, which is the Way of final knowing. Now that you have achieved maturity of preparation, you should renounce your merely preparatory practices, which are all based upon the need for counter-effort, to actively transcend the previously acquired ego-habit of turning outward, into the space of the world. Therefore, you should relinquish your Yogic practices of meditation—that direct (and, thereby, support) the mind (via prayers, mantras, and inwardly perceived phenomenal conditions) toward mere ideas, or toward otherwise conditionally perceived forms within, and, altogether, toward the conceptual and perceptual myth of "God". Instead of such beginner's practices, you should practice <u>constant</u> turning, away from body and mind, and (thus and thereby) toward and to Self-Abiding <u>as</u> the intrinsic State (or mere Self-Awareness) of Consciousness <u>itself</u>.

24. All the constituents of the conditionally apparent cosmic world are interdependently connected, in a unified field of causes and effects. The true Realizer of final knowing directly transcends the totality of cosmic existence, from the lowest order of things and beings to the cosmically pervasive Spirit-energy that is (itself) the merely-seeming light that shifts the universe in time. That all-transcending Way is the practice done prior to the cosmic universe of material light. It is the exercise of final knowing, prior to causes and effects. It is the Way of the underlying Reality—the Way of merely Self-Abiding, <u>as</u> Consciousness <u>itself</u>.

25. The mind of "point of view" is restless in its seeming space of time—like a monkey on the inside of a human head. If the monkey is disciplined from all its wandering, and, at last, is held firm in the

non-conditional Space of Consciousness itself—perfect true liberation is immediately (and inherently) achieved.

26. The intrinsically Self-Evident Self-Awareness of Consciousness itself
    <u>is</u> the one, indivisible, non-dual Reality that is underlying and pervad-
    ing the cosmic totality—prior to the body, and prior to the mind.

27. That Which is one and only, indivisible and non-dual, and prior to
    all is, itself, formless, non-conditional, and non-"objective"—and,
    yet, like space itself, it pervades all beings and all things in the cos-
    mic whole. Anyone who Self-Abides in the underlying Bliss <u>is</u> that
    Bliss <u>itself</u>. What is merely Reality is wonderful to know!

28. The constant motion of the mind will inevitably come to rest—if
    it is deprived of "<u>objects</u>" (much as a fire will extinguish itself, if its
    fuel no longer happens to the flame).

29. Understand this: Perfect true liberation requires the transcending
    of <u>all</u> conditional states—all of desire, all seeking, all illusions, all
    "mystical swooning", even all of waking, all of dreaming, and all of
    sleeping, too.

30. If the Self-radiance (or intrinsic and inherently perfect Spirit-
    energy) of Self-existing Consciousness (itself) is distinguished (or
    purified and released) from apparent association with the gross
    body, the thinking mind, the active intelligence, and the very "point
    of view" that is the ego-"I"—then inherent identification with Self-
    existing and Self-radiant Consciousness <u>itself</u> is (thus and thereby)
    achieved.

31. By a combination of inattention and restlessness, the mind becomes
    undisciplined—and, thus and thereby, the ego-fool increases, and
    the usual destiny of every bad result comes following the ego-mind.

Therefore, one must always remain alert, to always control the egoic wandering of thoughts—and, at last, by means of the exercise of the Way of final knowing, one must be always turned about, to Self-Abide as the intrinsic Self-Condition of Consciousness itself. The practitioner of the Way of final knowing must always persist in this final discipline of the mind—returning it, moment to moment, to the underlying native State that is Consciousness itself.

32. When the mind is steadily at rest in the underlying Self-Condition, it should be left at rest—and not exercised for any reason. There is no purpose to be served in the underlying Self-Condition by stimulating the efforts of thinking, doubting, and problem-solving. Therefore, sink the mind in the underlying State, of Self-Awareness of Consciousness itself—and leave it there.

33. The mind always seeks "objects" of sense-perception and of conceptual thinking—in order to support its would-be-persistent activity. Therefore, always undermine the event of mind, by depriving it of "objects". De-activate the mind, by cutting off its "fuel supply"—and do not stir the "embers", but let the mind dissolve to no more motions, in the non-"objective" peace of only-Consciousness (itself).

34. Relinquish the mind in the prior Self-Consciousness, Which always pervades even all conditionally arising "objects" and events, but Which, nevertheless, is not (at any time) limited by any "objects" of any kind—just as the space in which apparently material "objects" arise is not touched by any "objects" at any time (and neither is it emptied by their disappearance).

35. When the real and right practice of the Way of final knowing establishes perfect true liberation, by dissolution of the mind in its Source-Condition (Which is Consciousness itself), the inherent ultimate purpose of human birth is perfectly and finally fulfilled. In

this manner, even every kind of search for knowledge is inherently and truly perfectly satisfied.

36. In the practice of the Way of final knowing, Yogic meditation on the spinal "kundalini chakras" and the energy centers in the brain is to be entirely relinquished. All such psycho-physical (or merely conditional) Yogic meditations merely fuel (and, thereby, support) the mind with "objects"—whereas the practice of the Way of final knowing requires the perfect deprivation of the mind, by turning it from all possible "objects" (both internal and external).

37. As a preliminary (and otherwise ordinary remedial) discipline, if the mind becomes inattentive and stupefied, one must discipline it with alert attentiveness—and, if the mind wanders, one must bring it back to a one-pointed focus. The greater discipline than this ordinary (or merely preliminary) practice of mind-responsibility is that of the Way of final knowing, wherein there is neither stupefaction nor motion of mind—but there is merely Self-Abiding, prior to mind, in and <u>as</u> the intrinsically Self-Evident Self-Condition of Consciousness (<u>itself</u>).

38. That perfect true liberation inherently established by merely Self-Abiding <u>as</u> the Self-Evident State of final knowing is inherently prior to all "objects", and, therefore, inherently free of mind—because neither any "objects" nor the mind itself exist in the Self-Evident State of Consciousness <u>itself</u>.

39. Having renounced all the "object"-oriented paths of desire and seeking, be established firmly in the primary "location"—the Transcendental Seat of the heart, prior to the mind. Then (or on that underlying foundation), persist in the fundamental practice of the Way of final knowing—<u>there</u>, at heart. Do this until the Self-existing and Self-radiant Self-Awareness of Consciousness itself Shines heart-Awake, with immense fullness and lucidity.

40. Know this: Whoever is really and truly turned upon the intrinsically Self-Evident Self-Awareness of Consciousness (itself)—such that, by constant right practice, true and stable Self-Abiding as That is established—will (thus, and by virtue of the Self-existing and Self-radiant State of Consciousness alone) really and finally transcend and go beyond this world of birth, and change, and suffering, and death.

41. All that is apparently "objective"—whether by perception or conception—is, as such, not-Self. All "objects", all that is "objectified", or defined by relatedness, or apparent as an "other", and, indeed, all knowing of "objects", others, or relations of any kind—including any and every kind of "God"-Other, or any and every kind of "objectified gods", or any and every kind of "objectified goddesses", and even any and every kind of purposive or goal-oriented activity, directed toward the fulfillment of any and every kind of search at all—all of that becomes only more bondage, attachment, illusion, and suffering. Only Self-Realization, by Self-Abiding as That Which is intrinsically Self-Evident as the true and very Self—or as That Which always already Stands in the Self-Position, and as the intrinsically Self-Evident Self-Condition, prior to any and all possible "objectification" or "otherness" or relatedness—is perfect true liberation from all bondage.

42. All possible "objects" are characterized, experientially, by polar oppositions of positive and negative qualities—"yes" and "no", pleasurable and painful, good and bad, gain and loss, and so on. When all polarized "pairs" (or opposites) are transcended, the Truth of Reality is finally known. The Realizer of such final knowing is a perfect Yogi—truly liberated from all bondage.

43. The perfect Yogi, who has—by means of final-knowing-only— Realized perfect true liberation from all bondage, does not seek to

dissociate from the body while alive. In the case of such a Realizer, the body comes to the end of its lifetime in due course, when the previous actions that caused it even to be born have exhausted their momentum. However, such a Realizer—knowing the true Self-Condition is, inherently, both egoless and actionless—has already ceased to be the interested cause of actions and results that would look to produce embodiments beyond the present lifetime.

44. Self-existing Consciousness (itself), Self-radiant in the heart, is inherently non-conditional (and utterly free of conditioning) and inherently actionless (or non-causative). When Self-existing and Self-radiant Consciousness (itself) Self-absorbs (or dissolves) the ego-"I" into the true (inherently egoless) Self-Condition (of Consciousness itself)—perfect true liberation is (thus and thereby) Given by Divine Grace. This is my assurance to you.

45. Therefore, finally renounce and transcend all of your bondage to "objects", others, and dualities—by practicing the exercise of final knowing, which is perfect devotional yielding to the State of non-different Self-Identification with inherently actionless, inherently non-conditional, and inherently egoless Consciousness <u>itself</u>.

46. In the right practice of the Way (or exercise) of final knowing, you must forget (or cease to be concerned about) all that otherwise defines you in the world—such as your nationality, your politics, your status in community, your business, your family, your intimate relatedness, or, as the case may be, your status as a renunciate. The only practice relevant to the Way (or exercise) of final knowing is that of yielding to the State of non-different Self-Identification with the intrinsically Self-Evident Self-Condition of Consciousness <u>itself</u>.

47. "I am Consciousness itself. I am Consciousness-only. I am inherently relationless—neither owned nor owning. I am one and only." Such is the inherent heart-affirmation to be tacitly exercised and intrinsically Realized.

48. The Realizer of perfect true liberation is one who is tacitly exercised in the Way of final-knowing-only—whereas anyone who is exercising a contrary or lesser (or otherwise merely preliminary and conditional) path is yet in bondage to "objects" and conditions.

49. The instant the heart truly and finally re-discovers "I am not the body—I am intrinsically Self-Evident Consciousness itself", all bondage to desire and seeking vanishes, and perfect true liberation is achieved.

50. Thus, the heart Realizes and affirms: "I am the one, and only, and all-pervading, and inherently formless, and perfectly non-conditional Self-Condition—intrinsically Self-Evident as Consciousness itself. Of This, there is no doubt in me.

51. "I am Consciousness itself, inherently free of all bondage, always already truly liberated, and perfectly indefinable—such that no thought can contain me, and no embodied entity or form can be separated from me (for all is only me). Therefore, I am inherently free from all possible sorrow.

52. "I am the intrinsically Self-Evident Self-Condition that is Consciousness itself, Self-existing, one, whole, complete, and deathless—inherently free of identification with the body (which is, in and of itself, not Consciousness itself, and not-Self). Therefore, I am not the bag of flesh, bounded between head and foot, with its 'insides' of breath, and energies, and emotions, and thoughts, and thinker, too—and ego's 'I' at root.

53. "I <u>am</u> That upon Which all who seek liberation are attending, by means of devotional contemplation and every kind of effort of meditation—but I <u>am</u> beyond and prior to all seeking-reach, even beyond and prior to the possible attainments associated with the common and merely conditional states, of waking, dreaming, and sleeping deep. I <u>am</u> That Which is senior to <u>all</u> conditional forms and beings—because I <u>am</u> the underlying substratum of the cosmic universe.

54. "I <u>am</u> That Which is worshipped by all who practice conventional (or merely exoteric) religion. I <u>am</u> That Which <u>is</u> the Subject That is celebrated in all religious ceremonies, and by means of all the religious kinds of sacrifices, and acts of penance, and good works. All who worship only worship <u>That</u> Which I <u>am</u>—even though they 'think' to worship <u>That</u> by many and various 'Divine Names', and via many and various 'Divine Forms', and on the basis of many and various 'Divine Myths'.

55. "Everyone who practices religiously motivated, or even only morally motivated, disciplines and well-intended good works, only—thus and thereby—worships (or, otherwise, intends toward) <u>That</u> Which I <u>am</u>. Wherever actions are performed, even for whatever reason at all, only <u>That</u> Which I <u>am</u> <u>is</u> there and then—and <u>is</u> the why and how and what and who it <u>is</u>. I <u>am</u> That Which <u>is</u> the one and only and infinite and Self-Evidently Divine Condition that <u>is</u> Reality.

56. "I am not the gross (or outward) body. I am not the subtle (or inward) body. I am not the causal (or root) body. I <u>am</u> That Which is of the nature of Transcendental knowledge—beyond and prior to all that is conditionally known. I <u>am</u> That Which is beyond and prior to the cosmic universe, and Which is beyond and prior to the common conditional states (of waking, dreaming, and sleeping). I <u>am</u> That Which <u>is</u> eternal, infinite, free, and Self-Evidently Divine."

57. Consciousness <u>itself</u> is non-conditional, not-born, complete in itself, formless, relationless, worldless, "objectless", and without bondage of any kind. Consciousness <u>itself</u> cannot be compared to anything that is presumed to be other than (or different from) Consciousness <u>itself</u>. Consciousness <u>itself</u> cannot be contained, or defined, or analyzed, or comprehended, or in any manner "objectified" (or even noticed) by the mind. Consciousness <u>itself</u> cannot be heard, or seen, or tasted, or smelled, or touched, or felt at all, or in any manner or by any means perceived by the senses, or the sense-mind, or the body-mind. Nevertheless, Consciousness <u>itself</u> always already Self-Abides (Self-existing and Self-radiant) in its Transcendental Seat, at and prior to and beyond the heart-root.

58. Whoever consistently heart-affirms and (thus) tacitly knows the Supreme Self-Condition of Reality truly becomes That—<u>thus</u> Realizing That, by Self-Abiding <u>as</u> That-only. Whoever fulfills the whole course—from understanding That, to meditating on That, and, finally, to Self-Abiding <u>as</u> That—Realizes the deathless State of That-alone.

59. In response to your earnest request to be instructed in the knowledge of the Way by which true liberation may be attained, I have thoroughly explained to you, and to all, the Way of final knowing. Now, in response to your additional honorable request for instruction in the details of the practice whereby true liberation may be attained, I will speak further, about matters of discipline—for the sake of everyone who would know and practice it.

60. For those who, by means of right life and meditation, have become prepared to practice the Way of final knowing, the orientation (and, indeed, the necessity) of all preparatory practices has been fulfilled. Therefore, what was necessary in order to become prepared is no longer necessary—or even appropriate—as a means for the attain-

ing of perfect true liberation through the practice of the Way of final-knowing-only.

61. Therefore, conventional religious observances are not for those who practice the Way of final knowing. Religious piety, prayers, the study of Scriptural texts intended for beginners, programs of invocation, and of repetitions of sacred words, and of deity-worship, pilgrimages, sacred paraphernalia, and merely formalistic rules of all kinds—no such practices, or rules, or associations have further use, when the Way of final knowing is truly and rightly exercised.

62. One who truly and rightly practices the Way of final-knowing-only does not engage in activities for the purpose of causing any results that might be presumed to have relevance to either final knowing or perfect true liberation. The specific practice of the Way of final knowing involves no conditional exercises, no purposive acts, no modes of conduct that are intended to produce results, or to achieve benefits or merits, of any kind at all.

63. Therefore, anyone who is truly and rightly prepared to practice the Way of final knowing must enter into that discipline by renouncing all previous religious vows and practices, all that constitutes a prescriptive and purposive plan of action, all of seeking toward goals of any kind at all. All action causes results—and all results, or conditions of any kind, are (in and of themselves) bondage. In the Way of final knowing—which is the Way of perfect true liberation from all bondage—the characteristic renunciation (or right discipline) required (or that is inherently necessary) is the renunciation of seeking, or of conditional and purposive (or goal-oriented) action, effort, or method.

64. If anyone enters the Way of final knowing having already acquired supernormal powers or demonstrably unique psychic abilities, all

seeking to persist in the exercise of those powers or abilities should be relinquished—and all mental attachment to the supernormal and psychic demonstrations of the "secrets of cosmic nature" should be renounced.

65. All exercises of supernormal powers and unique psychic abilities are merely the more "advanced" forms of indulgence in purposive activity—or seeking toward results and goals. Therefore, all such activities—like even all more ordinary modes of seeking-activity—merely lead to more bondage, and to the general intensification of egoity, and even to low-mindedness. The Reality-Joy of perfect true liberation is not in any action, or in any seeking, or in any results, or in any goals at all—but only in perfect Self-Abiding as the inherently perfect State of Self-existing and Self-radiant Consciousness itself.

66. In the Way of final knowing, the Yoga of true Self-Abiding must be the one and only and constant practice, under all conditions—and without becoming otherwise conformed to any conditions, or any modes of activity. Therefore, if—due to past practices, or past associations—old habits or impulses or practice-tendencies arise, they should be immediately rejected.

67. The practitioner of the Way of final knowing should, characteristically, maintain a disposition of true equanimity—steadily, under all conditions, without seeking, without clinging attachments, and without fear. Merely by persistent true Self-Abiding as the inherently perfect Self-Condition of Consciousness itself, be a perfect Yogi.

68. Merely by persistent true Self-Abiding as the inherently perfect Self-Condition of Consciousness itself, solitude is constantly established as the one and only circumstance—and the Self-existing Self-radiance of Reality itself Shines greatly, even in the living body.

69. Perfect true liberation is achieved <u>only</u> by means of the tacit exercise of final (or intrinsic, and inherently perfect) knowing. No merely conditional (or, in any manner or kind, psycho-physical) means or activities of <u>any</u> kind can achieve perfect true liberation—because perfect true liberation is mere (or intrinsic, and intrinsically perfect and true) Realization of the intrinsic Self-Condition of Consciousness <u>itself</u>. Consciousness (<u>itself</u>) cannot be caused. Therefore, perfect true liberation cannot be achieved as a result of any kind of conditional or purposive activity—or by means of any kind or method of seeking at all.

70. The true Self-Realized Sage—who always Self-Abides <u>as</u> the intrinsic Self-Condition of Self-existing and Self-radiant Consciousness (<u>itself</u>)—should always be approached, with true devotion, for Blessing-Grace. Those who do this (and who remain constantly turned toward the Sage, worshipping the Sage with all the faculties of the body-mind) are Given the many Gifts of right instruction—and, in due course, they are Spiritually and Divinely Blessed with the heart-Transmission of the perfectly Self-Abiding State of Transcendental Self-Awakening. This is a Great Secret, fully understood and most truly valued only by true (and even most mature) devotees.

71. Now, I have Revealed to you, and to all, the Way of final knowing <u>and</u> the summary of its necessary discipline—as you asked me to do. The Way of final knowing is the Way whereby perfect true liberation is achieved—by means of resort to the Blessing-Grace of a true Self-Realized Sage. Therefore, the Way of final knowing is named the "Way of knowledge that becomes possible only at the final stage of maturity".

72. Have you any further questions?

X

REALITY (ITSELF) IS ALL THE GOD THERE IS

✢

A Discourse Given by Avatar Adi Da Samraj to His devotees, on January 6, 2006—directly after He had first Recited His Rendering of the Devikalottara

1.

A principal aspect of this book is to offer My English-language Renderings of texts from the sixth stage (or non-dualist) tradition, the tradition of the Advaitic and Buddhist Sages. The texts as they are presented here by Me could be called "translations"—yet, they are not translations in the conventional sense (that is, in the sense of a professional scholar making relatively literal renderings, in English, of pre-existing texts that were written or spoken in a different language). There can be no such thing as a literal translation of such traditional texts as these, principally because these texts were not written in plain (or conventional) speech. In addition, they were written a very long time ago. How long ago cannot exactly be determined, and it is different in each case—but, taken together, as a group, these texts were written between one thousand (give or take a few hundred years) and two thousand (or, in the case of Gotama Sakyamuni, even more[1]) years ago. Furthermore, although there exist conventional English translations of these texts, representing an effort to make a relatively literal presentation—because the texts themselves were not constructed on the basis of English grammar, they cannot, if they are to be rightly and fully understood, be presented in a mere word-for-word translation. Rather, any so-called "translation" must be an interpretation.

The conventions of making translations of traditional esoteric (Spiritual and Transcendental) texts are such that, typically, the translations are not done by Realizers—and, in many cases, not even by practitioners. Inevitably, if the rendering is made by someone who has not Realized the Truth of the text, then the translation—or the interpretation—will not have Realization as its basis. The presentation of a text of Reality-Teachings is a matter of Teaching Reality to listeners. Therefore, the right communication of such a text must be done on the basis of the Realization of Reality Itself. Typically, however, the translations of traditional texts are made by professional scholars, or people who (for whatever reasons) have an "objectified" interest in the material. The typical approach is to provide a relatively literalistic (and, as such, "correct") version of the text, but—because of the inevitable obscuration of meaning that is the result of literalistic, and merely mind-based, and ego-based, translation "methods"—the reader is also supplied with copious footnotes, and elaborately explanatory commentaries that may be many, many times longer than the original text.

If Realization is true of the translator, then the Truth of any text can be re-spoken—or spoken now, in present time. Only in that case can the texts be made to fully speak the Truth, the meanings in the texts having been rightly located and rendered in language that is comprehensible. Fully, rightly done, the rendering of the text should (in such a case) not require extensive (or even any) further commentary. The text should be plainly spoken—and made to speak plainly—just as it is. Footnotes should (in general) not be much required. Therefore, My Renderings of traditional texts in this book are plainly spoken, and they are Freely Speaking the Truth of the original texts.

Ancient texts typically contain obscure references—local, provincial references, cultural references belonging to the time and the place in which the text was made—which, often, are elements that have virtually no use for simply transmitting the meanings of the text. It is necessary, then, that the texts be re-spoken, from their original (and non-provincial) depths of meaning—and, thus, be spoken truly, and only effectively, as if for the first time. Therefore, I have Spoken these texts Myself—by Means of a Perfect Identification with the texts themselves, in the Source-Position of the Realization at the root of each text, and in the Self-Position of the Realizer (or, as the case may be, the Realizers, the practitioners, and the entire serious tradition) at the origin of each text.

2.

Each of the first six (or developmental) stages of life suffers from a characteristic limitation. The "point of view" of each of the six developmental stages of life involves egoic "self"-identification with a particular psycho-physical characteristic (or state, or dimension) of the total (gross, subtle, and causal) structure of the body-mind-complex.

The sixth stage approach suffers from its particular perspective (or "point of view", or "method"), just as all the other developmental stages do. The text of the *Devikalottara,* for example, speaks (at times) of a kind of "inversion-method" for achieving Realization. There is also reference to preliminary "methods" of various kinds, some of which are communicated explicitly (or rather directly suggested) as prerequisites for "the Way of Final Knowing" (as I phrase it in My Rendering of the text of the *Devikalottara*).

The principal admonition in the *Devikalottara* is to turn (or invert) the mind toward its Source. In other words, there is a particular admonition in this text that carries with it the limitation of traditional strategic (and, necessarily, psycho-physical) "method". Even though the text argues against such matters, some kind of strategic "method" is yet being suggested. There are even earlier preliminary "methods", and that fact is also made clear. Yet, even in relation to "the Way of Final Knowing", there is a kind of strategic "method" that is prescribed as a preliminary to actual "Final Knowing", and which is the "method" of turning (or inverting) the mind toward its Source (or in other words, turning attention toward Consciousness Itself).

This "method" (of turning the mind toward its Source) is (itself) a not-yet-Perfect practice. It is a "method" of the exclusionary turning of the faculties <u>away</u> from their "objects" (or away from the "world") and <u>toward</u> their Source-Position (or the Consciousness-Position). This is the principal traditional sixth stage "method". There are other sixth stage "methods" as well—yet, this is the fundamental one. That "method", that action, that intention, is yet a limitation—although it is a (necessarily, only preliminary, and conditional) turning toward That Which <u>Is</u> (Inherently) Non-Dual, Indivisible, or One. There is no second to That One. There is no "other". There are no "objects". There is simply That Reality Which <u>Is</u> Consciousness Itself.

On the one hand, That Principle <u>Is</u> Truth. On the other hand, the "method" of turning upon It is a "method" of exclusion. That "method" is yet based on the "root"-disposition that is egoity itself. Therefore, there is a limitation in that "method"—the limitation of tacitly feeling that one fundamental affirmation, that turning upon the Transcendental Source-Condition (or Consciousness Itself), affirming that one is only That, rather than one or another conditional state. Any such strategic turning—and, indeed, any continued exercising of any kind of conditional (or psycho-physical) "method"—even though it can be said to have some kind of virtue in the course of the approach to Perfect practice, is not yet (or itself) Perfect practice.

That Which Is (Ultimately) to be Realized Is Inherently One, not Two. That Which Is (Ultimately) to be Realized Is Non-Dual and Indivisible—and It cannot be Realized by any conditional (or psycho-physical) means. It cannot be Realized by the inversion of the faculties. It can only be <u>Inherently</u> Realized. It is (necessarily) only Self-Established. In Its Most Perfect Realization (in the Awakening to the seventh stage of life), there is no turning. There is simply Self-Abiding <u>As</u> That.

There is some premonitory foreshadowing of the seventh stage Realization in the traditional texts presented herein, but the traditional texts characteristically suggest that Realization is attained by a "method" of turning or of being released from mind (or the total body-mind-complex). The "method" for achieving such release previous to Perfect Realization Itself is the sixth stage "method". It is a "method" that turns upon What Is One and Indivisible—but, because that turning is exclusionary, the "root"-characteristic of egoity is still intact.

Truly Perfect practice involves no turning, no "method" applied to the body-mind-"self". The only-by-Me Revealed and Given "Perfect Practice" of the Reality-Way of Adidam is not associated with any "method". The "Perfect Practice" of the Reality-Way of Adidam is Self-Established, Transcendentally Spiritually Given by My Divine Avataric Transcendental Spiritual Blessing-Transmission. The process of the only-by-Me Revealed and Given Reality-Way of Adidam is a Transcendental Spiritual process. Nevertheless, the Ultimate (or Perfect) process of the Reality-Way of Adidam is not an exercise of the body-mind-"self" (or an exercise of the faculties). There is no longer any "method" of any kind. There is only Transcendental (and, most ultimately, Divine) Self-Abiding (Itself). That Self-Abiding is not established philosophically, not merely thought about and somehow affirmed, somehow located. That Self-Abiding is Spiritually and Transcendentally Established.

The Teachings of the Sages carry within them the final limitation that exists within the Great Tradition of humankind as a whole, and it is the sixth stage error. The only-by-Me Revealed and Given seventh stage Awakening specifically requires the transcending of the sixth stage error. In fact, the seventh stage Awakening requires the transcending of the errors of all of the six developmental stages of life. The seventh stage Awakening involves the Prior transcending of egoity itself. Such transcending is not a philosophical matter, not something that can be settled here and now—in a discussion, for instance. This much can be said of it: that the ego-transcending process is required. My Divine Avataric Blessing-Grace is required. Your devotion to Me is required. Surrender of separate and separative "self" is required. Counter-egoic practice is required.

In the course of preparing to enter into the "Perfect Practice" of the Reality-Way of Adidam, there are disciplines of various kinds that effectively deal with the wandering of attention, the wandering of mind, the wandering of the body-mind-"self", or the wandering in the body-mind-"self". When such wandering is so intensely engaged that there is no freedom from it, the Perfect (or truly Real-God-Realizing) process is not yet possible.

The purpose of the preliminaries of practice (or the earlier demonstration of practice) in the only-by-Me Revealed and Given Reality-Way of Adidam (and also in the traditional setting) is (as it is said in the traditional texts herein Rendered by Me) to bring about a cessation of the mind, to control the mind perfectly—or, in other words, to control the total body-mind-complex of egoity, bondage, or seeking. Only when the patterning of the body-mind-complex is sufficiently undone—such that the Grace of My Transcendental Spiritual Transmission can Awaken the Realization of the Self-Evidently Divine Self-Nature, Self-Condition, and Self-State (in Place)—can the "Perfect Practice" of the Reality-Way of Adidam begin. Only then is the "Perfect Practice" Established and (thereby) begun. The same Consciousness That is declared in the sixth stage tradition is Declared by Me, in the seventh stage (or truly Most Perfect) Manner. It is simply that, in the sixth stage tradition, there is an inversion upon That Which Is One—and, therefore, there is (it may be said) a mode of dualism yet. Whereas, when I am Speaking to you, when I am making My Divine Avataric Self-Confession to you, and I am using the term "Consciousness", I am not speaking in terms of any conditional means whatsoever for Realizing It or for keeping It in place. I am Speaking It simply. In the only-by-Me Revealed and Given seventh stage Awakening, Consciousness is Self-Evident. It is Priorly and Most Perfectly Established—Beyond all doubt, Beyond all limitations, Beyond all "methods". The apparently arising "world" is Divinely Self-Recognized. The apparently arising "world" is not a "something" that must be escaped. It is not a "something" that is an inherent problem—because it is Divinely Self-Recognized.

Until there is the most perfect transcending of egoity, the "world" is not Divinely Self-Recognized. The "world" is found to be "other" than Consciousness, and that (false, or limited) presumption is the source of the limitation that is characteristic of the sixth stage tradition. On the basis of this presumption, the "world" is yet a problem. The "world" is not Divinely Self-Recognized. Rather, the "world" is presumed to be other than the Transcendental Self-Condition. This presumption (or limitation) is fundamental both to the Buddhist tradition and to the tradition of Advaitism.

One of the principal declarations said to have been made by Gotama Sakyamuni is that a fundamental characteristic of conditional arising is that it is "not-self". Therefore, the practice in the Buddhist tradition is to work to overcome the tendency to cling to what is "not-self", to be bound to what is "not-self". When that bondage is purified or relinquished, then That Which Is not born—and Gotama affirmed that there Is the Unborn—Is Self-Evident.

Because of this characteristic doctrine of "not-self" (or the idea that no configuration of conditions constitutes a separate and permanent "self"), the capitalized term "Self" is not used in the Buddhist tradition to describe the Transcendental Reality. Nevertheless, the Realization or Reality referred to in the Buddhist tradition Is the very same Realization or Reality that is declared in the tradition of Advaitism by using the capitalized term "Self". In the tradition of Advaitism, the term "Self" (with a capital "S") does not mean an "entity within", or a separate being. Rather, the capitalized term "Self", as used in the Advaitic tradition, Is What in the Buddhist tradition is otherwise described as "the Unborn"—"no mind", not a "self", not the separate "atman" (or the individual "self"), but only That "Atman" Which Is "Brahman".

"Nirvana" and "Brahman" are the same (or Not-"different"). The Realization of "Nirvana" Is the Realization of "Brahman". The two words ("Nirvana" and "Brahman") are forms of technical language, each specific to a particular tradition of discourse. "Nirvana" is Non-conditional, Not-born, Not-separate, Not-a-"self", Not-"caused", and

Not-"causable"—but "It" <u>Is</u> the Acausal, Transcendental, Perfectly Prior Self-Condition (or Intrinsic Condition) of all conditionally apparent events, forms, beings, and states. That is to say, "Nirvana" <u>Is</u> "Brahman". The Realization of "Brahman" <u>Is</u> "Nirvana". The Inherently "Nirvanic" State of "Brahman" <u>Is</u> the Non-separate Condition of <u>all</u> apparent conditions. Therefore, as stated in the "Mahayana" tradition of Buddhism: "Nirvana" (or the Non-conditional) and "samsara" (or all that is conditional) <u>Are</u> the same (or Not-"different"). Non-"difference" <u>Is</u> Reality <u>Itself</u>.

Therefore, both Buddhism and Advaitism—the two principal sixth stage traditions—are speaking of the same Realization. Nevertheless, the institutionally competitive advocates of the two traditions differentiate themselves from (and argue with) one another, and, thereby, propound a difference—and they have done so for thousands of years.

What I have to Say about this apparent disagreement is that there <u>is</u> <u>no</u> <u>difference</u>. That is why <u>both</u> Buddhist and Advaitic texts are included herein, by Me. The texts presented in this book contain criticisms of the conventionally "religious" disposition, criticisms of conventional "religious" practices, and criticisms of systems of conventional "religious" belief. Even esoteric Spiritual practice is criticized in these traditional texts, in the form of a criticism of all kinds of Yogic techniques and "methods"—indicating that such "methods" are preliminary, or only preparatory, and no longer necessary at the Ultimate stage. However, the modes of <u>exoteric</u> "religion" are criticized as being <u>completely</u> without relevance in relation to Ultimate Realization. The exoteric practices are described as being (at best) modes of practice for beginners. In the *Ribhu Gita,* for example, Ribhu goes to town again and again to see if His devotee Nidagha is still practicing the conventional exoteric "religious" piety of a serious temple-goer, believing and praying and worshipping in the context of the exoteric "religious" society and culture of his village. Ribhu is finally able to move Nidagha beyond such exotericism—toward the Way of "Perfect Knowledge".

In the *Devikalottara,* such preliminary practices—including adherence to "God"-ideas and "God"-myths, and participation in "religious" activities (not only temple activities and praying, but also the "religiously"-motivated moral activities, or presumed-to-be moral activities, that are characteristically associated with much of "religious" idealism)—are said to have no relevance whatsoever to "Perfect Knowledge". In fact, such practices are described as counter-productive— because they simply produce ego-binding "results", in the form of more "objects", more conditions, and (therefore) more bondage. Such practices may be well-intended, and they may have their place in the ordinary "world" of egos. In the ordinary "world" of egos, "religious" myths are presumed to be not myths but Reality. However, from the perspective of the Realization of Reality Itself, they are understood to be myths— just that, a product of childish mind, of beginner's ego-mind.

Conventional "religion" is largely about idealizing social behaviors. In fact, conventional "religion" could be described as the mythology of human social behavior. There exists a great deal of mythology and beliefs and temple activities and paraphernalia—but, when all of that is understood, it becomes clear that the fundamental purpose of the myths, the stories, and the beliefs is simply to reinforce what is regarded to be positive social behavior.

Thus, the Divine is not what is fundamental to conventional "religion". In conventional "religion", the Divine Reality is mythologized— not Realized. What is fundamental to conventional "religion" is social concern. Conventional "religion" is a "method", in other words, for attempting to maintain a positive social order. Of course, conventional "religion" never succeeds in any perfect sense—any more than sheerly political "methods" for achieving a positive social order ever achieve perfection (or the desired utopia).

Nevertheless, despite the impossibility of any such "success", the fundamental nature of conventional "religion" is socially based (and socially purposed) activity. Thus, conventional "religion" essentially belongs to the collective domain of humanity, rather than to the Core (or Source-Domain of Ultimate Realization). By contrast, the modes of esotericism lead in the <u>direction</u> of that Source-Domain, but only "Perfect Knowledge" of That Which Is Inherently Perfect is (Most Ultimately) Divine Self-Realization.

The name "God"—and, altogether, the reference to the Divine in the form of myths—is a habit of mind. When there is Divine Self-Realization, there is no mind whatsoever. When there is Divine Self-Realization, there are no habits of mind and, therefore, no myths of "God". The myths and "God"-ideas are out-grown. They are unnecessary—and, in fact, they are relinquished, because it is understood that (ultimately) they are part of the bondage of ego-mind.

That does not mean that a positive human disposition is regarded to be inappropriate. In fact, such virtues are regarded to be absolutely necessary at the foundation, as preparation for the Ultimate practice. However, the mythological basis for "religious" seeking—the "religious" (or mythological) conceptualization of life—is specifically criticized in the tradition of the Reality-Teachings of the Sages.

What about the myths of "Reality" that are proposed by advocates of the scientific view of existence, rather than the "religious" view? I have Described such advocates as being adolescents (compared to those who, being conventionally "religious" rather than scientific, are more childish in their disposition). The adolescent is caught between the motive to be dependent and the motive to be independent.

A myth of "Reality" is upheld by the scientific view in its conventional form (as scientific materialism). The scientific "method" (itself) is simply a mode of inquiry, useful within a certain sphere of possibility—but the culture of science (or the "cult" of science, or the tradition of science), like the tradition of conventional "religion", is based upon certain propositions, certain limitations of view based on egoity.

Like conventional "religion", the scientific view (in its conventional form) is confined to the domain of the first three stages of life—to the body orientation, or the body "point of view"—except that the orientation of science is adolescent by comparison to the childish orientation of conventional "religion".

The view of science is very much oriented toward the myth of "matter"—and, yet, such is a rather archaic philosophical view. The notion of "matter" hardly applies anymore, even within the tradition of science. Science has become much too sophisticated. The concept of "matter" is a leftover from the nineteenth century, a leftover that persisted throughout the entire twentieth century. Since the time of Einstein and the developments of quantum theorizing, the idea that the "world" is "matter" is as archaic as the ancient notion that the "world" is made of earth, water, fire, air, and space. Indeed, by contrast, that ancient analysis of the constituents of the "world" is even more sophisticated than the view that the "world" is nothing but "matter".

What is "matter"? It is an absurd notion, a fixed idea, an uninspected idea (like the reference to "I" in conventional speech). Nobody has ever "experienced" so-called "matter". You do not "know" what "matter" is any more than you "know" what "I" is. Both "matter" and "I" are nonsense-terms that are used to justify an entire philosophy and a mode of control over the mind that (in fact) prevents greater comprehension. With relativity theory and quantum mechanics and much more, the entire notion of "matter" has become an absurdity.

I have suggested that the domain of science associated with quantum mechanics is actually an investigation of a level of cosmic reality that is (otherwise) noticed by human beings "subjectively". It is the realm in which not Consciousness Itself but conscious activities, conscious operations, are functioning at the deepest "subjective" level.

In the waking state, there is a perception of a certain degree of fixity, a "materiality" that is somehow rather stiff. However, when one enters into a somewhat deeper state—such as dreaming, and various other kinds of psychological states of some depth—that stiffness does not exist anymore. In such a state, it can be observed that all kinds of paradoxes are happening that appear to be illogical from the perspective of the waking state. Such paradoxes, which are now being observed in the field of quantum physics, are actually the paradoxes of the depth of the "world" in which human beings are participating. It is the "subjective" level of human participation, a dimension of conditionally apparent Reality that is utterly not (in any sense) predetermined and cannot, in fact, be determined even <u>after</u> the fact. That "subjective" realm is entirely indeterminate.

The paradoxical nature of Reality is not merely something weird happening out in space somewhere. There is a dimension within which the arising of cosmic existence is taking place, and which is not in the mode of the apparently stiff, rigid "materiality" of waking-state phenomena. Nevertheless, the "Reality" proposed by scientific materialism (or the general view of science) tends to bypass the implications of the discoveries that even science cannot deny. However, scientists tend to continue to argue about it, and not come to conclusions—such that they need not yet confront the implications of the paradoxes of the "world", and the fact that these paradoxes are no longer compatible with a materialistic philosophy.

The idea of "Reality" as "matter" is a myth, just as the conventional idea of "God" is a myth. The conventional idea of "God" is a myth that essentially justifies human social behaviors, while the idea of "Reality-as-matter" justifies a state of mind that is trapped in a struggle to achieve the power of unlimited control over the gross (physical) "world". Some scientists, for instance, argue about "consciousness". They generally define "consciousness" in terms of conscious operations (or functions)—and not as Consciousness <u>Itself</u>. Some, of course, raise the subject as a matter of discussion—to argue whether or not consciousness has some kind of transcendental status. However, even though some may examine this possibility, it is not really acceptable thinking or allowable "knowledge"—at least not yet—in the "world" of the adherents of scientific materialism.

Therefore, in the face of a wilderness of doctrines—"religious", scientific, every kind of doctrine, view, "point of view", idea, notion, interpretation of "experience" in the "world"—it was necessary that I find out. It is fundamental to My Divine Avataric Service here not to merely accept any "point of view" or doctrine or belief (of any kind whatsoever).

Therefore, in My Service to all beings, all views were Experienced, Suffered, and Relinquished (or Gone Beyond). I am not merely reporting a tradition about Consciousness. I did not merely "translate" the texts I am Presenting here. Realization Spoke these words—the Realization Proven by a Submission that is (Ultimately) without limitation. The Lifetime of This, My Body, has been a course of Submission, of Discipline, of Demonstration, more intense, and more profound, than any in the history of humankind—and utterly authentic, even in the basic manner of the true discipline of science.

The Truth communicated in the Teachings of the Sages—and, indeed, the Truth represented by every tradition (or "point of view")—was altogether found out, and noticed, by Me. And I have Communicated all of this to everyone, by Means of My Divine Avataric Demonstration (including My Revelatory Writings), such that the Unique Leela (or Divine History) of all My Divine Avataric Doings has taken tangible and communicative form.

The only-by-Me Revealed and Given Reality-Way of Adidam is Given by My Divine Avataric Blessing-Grace—and, therefore, the Reality-Way of Adidam is not replaceable by books or by any cultural or institutional means. That Gift is Mine to Do, now and forever. It is the responsibility of My devotees—and of everyone, now and in the future—to make use of Me for the Purpose of Divine Self-Realization, to be entered into the devotional (and, in due course, Transcendental Spiritual) relationship to Me for the sake of Realization (as a profound and serious matter).

Ultimately, the devotional relationship to Me becomes the "Perfect Practice" of the Reality-Way of Adidam. There are also practices that are preliminary practices, and those preliminary practices inherently transcend the various modes and "points of view" corresponding to egoic "self"-identification with the body, egoic "self"-identification with the mind (or the subtle dimension of egoity), and egoic "self"-identification with attention itself (or the "root"-dimension, or causal dimension, of egoity). Therefore, there are modes of practice in the only-by-Me

Revealed and Given Reality-Way of Adidam which I Describe as being preliminary to the "Perfect Practice". These modes of practice are necessary because of the bondage to "point of view"—the patterning of bondage with which each individual is associated—until there is a consistent going beyond that bondage of "point of view", that bondage to certain modes of structural identification with dimensions of the psycho-physical pattern of body-mind-"self" and its characteristic states.

Fundamentally, the preliminary practice in the Reality-Way of Adidam is the searchless practice of the tacit, direct, and intrinsic transcending of egoity itself. The "Perfect Practice", Itself, is Priorly (or Always Already) egoless—and, therefore, there is no active application of psycho-physical structures that is associated with the "Perfect Practice". The preliminary practice intensively transcends egoity—but the "Perfect Practice" has nothing to do with egoity.

Egoity is bondage to the "point of view" that identifies with modes of the structure of the body-mind-"self". When there is no exercise of the structures of the body-mind-"self" for the Purpose of Realization, there is also (necessarily) no egoity, no identification with the ego, no identification with the "self"-contraction of body-mind. This profound equanimity is a part of the necessary basis for the "Perfect Practice".

In any case, no matter what is arising, you are never in the position of that which is apparently arising. You are the Witness-Consciousness only. Consciousness Itself, Self-Existing and Self-Radiant, Is the Inherent Self-Position. When this becomes utterly clear—utterly—when there is no moving away from that Realization, then practice is Perfect and Liberation is Inherent and Absolute.

However, if you play in the "world" of your own "objects", if you play in the quantum illusions of your own psycho-physical fabrications, then there is no end to bondage. There is no end to "causes" and "effects", to "objects", to "results", to what is pulling you by the nose. The "world" just goes on and on and on.

And, then, all of a sudden, it seems it does not go on—but it is the same as when someone else dies and you have not made the transition yet. When someone else dies, you are yet standing in another location—and, therefore, it seems that the person has gone. In your own event, you will not (yourself) be left behind—but there is still the quantum domain of possibilities, which does not come to an end with death. Simply because there is a transition beyond physical life does not mean there is paradise. The transition beyond this life is not paradise. Death is a transition within the quantum domain of conditional existence—and that domain is everywhere based on the limitations that exist everywhere, in all planes, including this one.

When there is Most Perfect Awakening to the Self-Radiant Condition of Self-Existing Being, or True Divine Existence—not "God"-myth absorption, but True Divine Self-Realization—then there is utter freedom from the illusions of the imagined "worlds", the patterns that are developed out of chaos and that are suffered by everyone. Have a serious conversation with anyone, and you will find out that he or she is suffering. And so are you. Finding out the why and the how of it, and transcending that—that is the Ultimate process of life. That is the most serious course of life. There are various other modes of orientation, of course, some of which can be positively intended, but they are intended within a domain of limitations. Lesser choices have to do with bondage to lesser modes of "point of view" (or grades of energy, or vibration, of relative subtlety or grossness). There is the Realization, and there is the "radical" (or "at-the-root") Way of the Realization, that Perfectly Transcends all illusions, all suffering, and all bondage—and that is Perfectly Free in That Which Is Real (Acausal) God, rather than "God"-ideas (or "God"-myths) that are oriented toward modes of human mind and its limitations. Reality (Itself) Is all the God there Is. Reality Itself is not a myth, and It cannot be contained in mind—but It can be Realized.

Ideas of "God" as "causative", or "Creator", are ideas generated by human beings who are already identified with being a body-mind-"self" in the "world". In that circumstance, which is mortal, and extremely difficult for everyone, the ideas of the Divine that are generated are ideas based on that bondage, that attachment, that identification with the body-mind-"self". Thus, the Divine is thought of in a certain manner, in the modes of limitation. The "Creator-God" idea is a particular idea (or myth) of the Divine Reality (or of Reality Itself) just as the idea of "matter" is a myth of Reality Itself. These are conceptions of how things are, based on a presumed limitation, a "point of view", a "point of view" that has established modes of thinking and modes of living.

In a certain disposition, the limited presumption takes the form of conventional "religion". In another disposition, it takes the form of the scientific materialist's view of life. The many different modes of thinking are a very complex matter. Any particular individual is not one thing or another, but the individual is many, many things. Any individual arises and lives in the quantum "world" of paradoxes, in which (in any moment) a different characteristic is emphasized by conditions, by the desire-habit that has come to the front in the moment.

The "self"-presumed "person" is never an identifiable "somebody". Although the word "I" is used again and again and again, no actual (or quantifiable) referent is associated with the term. You use the term "I" as you use the terms "shirt" or "ceiling" or "light bulb"—as if "I" is just as straightforward a reference as "light bulb", or like a specific location on a map. No—the "I" is a myth. You do not actually have a quantifiable referent for the word "I". "I" is not a "someone", an identity that you have inspected, a particular quality or characteristic or anything that could be pointed to, even an "object" of some kind. "I" has no such reality.

When you say "I", you are not talking about anyone at all—really, no one at all. "I" is simply a convention of speech, around which all the referents of "experience" are categorized. The "I"-referent is nothing more than a form of tension (or contraction) of the entire structure of the body-mind-complex. There is no one who is the "I" to which you refer in speech hundreds of times every day. There is no such person. If you were to inspect it, you would see that there is no such person. "I" is a habit of the language itself—a piece of mere grammar. The internal and external "objects" surround and limit the "I"—but the "I" has no content otherwise.

People refer to "God" similarly, without inspecting what the word is supposed to be pointing to. There is no "God" that is actually "experienced". It is a conceptual construct that is really, in some sense, the mirror of the "I". It is not a quantifiable referent at all. It is just part of a larger construct of thinking that is associated with the feeling of separateness. There is no actually "experienced" ego-"self" (or "I") that is pointed to, or specifically referred to, by the use of the word "I". Rather, "I" is a word that is used within the context of a fundamental contraction, and all the modes of language in fact spin around that contraction.

There is much within the patterns of thinking that is not inspected. Mind is a pattern of conventions that is just carried around, uninspected, until it bumps up against "something", and you have to think about it—or else you find that "something" does not correspond to any reality at all, and then you must figure things out again.

Someone can be naively "religious" when young, and then (all of a sudden) the basis for "religion" is ripped away, because it was based on the essentially mythological assumptions of those who taught the young person the "religious" ideas. The myths were kinds of nursery-room stories, nursery-room myths given by adults to children, to you when you were a child—and you did not inspect them, because the process was not a process of thinking about anything. The stories were like the stories of Santa Claus, and like the nursery rhymes and mind-cartoons that are told to children, or to immature minds, and that are absorbed as part of the logic of how one lives. Perhaps it all makes sense in childhood, but when the child has become an adult, man or woman, he or she must put these childish things away and discover what is happening. You cannot depend on those myths. At some point, you must accept that there is no Santa Claus—and that there never was.

I assume you take it for granted that there is no Santa Claus, but perhaps you are more reluctant to be relieved of your childhood "religious" ideas about "God". You must find out about "God". The "God" of childhood is not real. The "God" posed by egoity is not real. Reality Is Real. Reality Is Divine. That Which Is Real God Is Acausal in Nature, not "causative"—Inherently actionless and Intrinsically egoless. The Divine Nature, Condition, and State to be Realized requires the transcending of egoity and all doings, all action, all bondage. That Which Is to be Realized—Reality Itself, That Which Is simply Self-Evident, Intrinsically the Case moment to moment—Is Identical to Consciousness Itself (or the Self-Existing and Self-Radiant Transcendental Spiritual Current of the Self-Apprehension of Being). Apart from the most profound and Most Perfect Realization of That, you have only a very superficial and "self"-deluded sense of What Consciousness Itself Is.

Reality Itself is not merely, "Oh, yes, the Awareness behind thinking." Reality Itself Is Divine. Reality Itself Is Absolute. It Is Infinite Force, "Brightness", Self-Radiant. All appearances are simply That. The Realization of Consciousness Itself is a profound Transcendental Spiritual and Divine Realization. Therefore, Realization is not simply about asserting some philosophical principle. Realization Is God-Realization, but It Is Realization of Real (Acausal) God, Which Is Reality Itself and not merely attachment to the myth of the Divine (which is basically attachment to the myth of ego-"I").

Ego-"I" makes a myth out of Reality and calls it any number of things—calls it "God", calls it "matter", calls it "sweetheart", whatever it calls it.

3.

DEVOTEE: Beloved Lord, in Your Rendering of the *Devikalottara,* You Say that the Way of "Perfect Knowledge" can be Realized by the Transmission of the Sage (or Realizer). Is this Your Own Revelation, rather than part of the original text?

AVATAR ADI DA SAMRAJ: No, I am Speaking of the tradition that has existed for thousands of years! Realization by the Blessing-Grace of a Realizer is the great secret of the Great Tradition of humankind. That is the ancient secret tradition. It has always been so. Therefore, it is specifically present in the *Devikalottara,* as well as in the other texts. I did not just add references about the Realizer and the Grace of the Realizer to these texts—these references exist in these texts themselves, and in many others.

What there Is to Realize is (potentially) limited only by the disposition of the devotee, and by the characteristics, the disposition, and the mode, or stage, of Realization of the Realizer. Therefore, My Gift to My devotees is the Gift of Most Perfect Realization, seventh stage Realization, through My Divine Avataric Work with them. That is part of the Unique Characteristic of My Divine Avataric Transcendental Spiritual Gift here. Yet, the process of devotion to the Realizer is most ancient, and it is the great secret—and, of course, it has been most fruitfully entered into only by a relative few.

Most of the Great Tradition consists of myths and programs of practice to be applied to oneself, philosophical talk of various kinds, techniques of all kinds. Yet, the core and great secret of the Great Tradition is Realization by Grace of the Realizer's Blessing in the course of living the relationship of devotional surrender to the Realizer, to the Master.

I did not Bring that principle to humanity for the first time. That is a part of what I am Manifesting here in full Coincidence with the Great Tradition. My Work is a Completing Work, or a Work at the most Full Point of the process that is potential for humankind. As it is said everywhere in the Great Tradition, when there is devotional resort, worshipping the Realizer with your entire being, when you truly surrender to a Master, then you are given Instruction. And, in due course, you are also given Realization, through direct—and, in the best of cases, Spiritual—Transmission.

There are dimensions to the Gift that I Bring here that can be seen in terms of both of those Gifts. There are Unique Characteristics to

My Divine Avataric Reality-Teaching, to the many modes of My Divine Avataric Teaching-Word. These Characteristics are truly Unique, and not found in the Great Tradition. Likewise, there is a Unique Dimension to My Divine Avataric Transcendental Spiritual Self-Transmission and Divine Avataric Awakening-Work. The process that is entered into (or, potentially, most fully Realized) by My devotees is that of the seventh stage Realization. That is another aspect of what I Bring here Uniquely—seventh stage Realization by Divine Avataric Transcendental Spiritual Blessing-Grace, and the Communication of the Unique and Complete Divine Avataric Way, the Teaching that accounts for the total process of Divine Self-Realization and for all aspects of responsibility that must be assumed by devotees if they would Realize Me.

Nevertheless, Realizers (in their various degrees) have passed on instructions and otherwise Blessed devotees with modes (or degrees) of Realization for thousands of years.

Of course, in My Renderings of traditional texts, it is I Who am Speaking via these texts. These are My Renderings, and so I am Illuminating the texts. Nevertheless, I have left the traditional Teachings (with even all their presumptions and limitations) intact in these texts. Each of the texts has elements that indicate the limitations of sixth stage traditions by comparison to the "Perfect Practice" of the Reality-Way of Adidam. I have left such elements in the texts—certain limitations in presumption or instruction, limitations otherwise in the sense of not being complete and not covering all kinds of details that have to do with what is really required as a preliminary, and what is really required in the context of the Perfect Demonstration of the Reality-Way. All kinds of elements are simply not there in these texts (which are otherwise Revealed by Me relative to the "Perfect Practice" of the Reality-Way of Adidam), and other kinds of things are stated in a limited fashion.

My "Perfect Practice" Reality-Teachings[2] illuminate the differences between the sixth stage traditions (as exemplified in these traditional texts) and the "Perfect Practice" of the Reality-Way of Adidam. I am not, however, presenting these traditional texts merely in order to criticize them. I am Speaking for the Great Tradition when I make these Renderings—and I am (thus) representing the Great Tradition as it is and in My Own Completing of it. The limitations in these texts are rather subtle—even difficult to notice. I am not setting up "straw men"—not at all. In fundamental terms, I Affirm and Uphold everything that is in these texts. You should—by means of serious study of My Divine Avataric Revelation-Word—be able to see how these traditional Reality-Teachings positively relate to the Reality-Way of Adidam, and particularly to the "Perfect Practice" of the Reality-Way of Adidam.

It is necessary that you see and understand the limitations of these traditions—but the limitations are not really in the form of them being "wrong". Rather, these traditional Reality-Teachings contain elements of what could be described as "preliminary practice", practice preliminary to the "Perfect Practice" as I have Described it. These traditional texts are not "wrong". They are outstanding among the greatest texts ever made!

XI

THE REALITY-TEACHINGS OF THE SAGE RIBHU

⁜

From the Ribhu Gita

1.

The Plain Truth of Traditional (or Sixth Stage) Non-Dualism, As Represented By The Ribhu Gita

The *Ribhu Gita* is one of the principal texts of the ancient sixth stage tradition of Non-Dualism (or "Advaitism")—and, as such, the *Ribhu Gita* itself stands as an exemplary epitome of the ancient traditional teachings of sixth stage Realizers, or "Sages".

The *Ribhu Gita* (literally, "Ribhu's Song") is Part Six of the *Siva Rahasya*—an ancient Asian Indian text, containing elements of myth, legend, and philosophy. The date of origin of the *Ribhu Gita* (itself) is uncertain—although it appears, from various conceptual and philosophical cues in the text, that it dates from sometime after the "Advaitic" Teacher Shankara (and, therefore, post eighth century CE). The *Ribhu Gita* is a presentation of traditional sixth stage Non-Dualist teachings, said to have been given to the Sage Ribhu by "God Himself", in the form of Lord Siva (the inherently Formless Divine Self-Reality, represented by a myth of Divine Personality, in and by Whom all beings and things are always priorly absorbed). The Sage Ribhu is, according to tradition, supposed to have given the teachings to His (at first, rather reluctant) devotee, Nidagha.

The *Ribhu Gita* itself is—by virtue of its summary of character-istics—effectively an epitome of the totality of sixth stage views and teachings of all the ancient non-dualist Realizers (or Sages). Chapter twenty-six of the *Ribhu Gita* is, itself, a summary statement that can be said to represent the totality of the *Ribhu Gita* as a whole. For this rea-son, chapter twenty-six is presented herein as the principal text of this intended epitome of the *Ribhu Gita* itself. Also, separately included (as a kind of preview of chapter twenty-six) are six additional verses, pre-sented herein as a summation of the "Essence" of the central teachings of the *Ribhu Gita* as a whole.

As a statement of Truth, the *Ribhu Gita* seems simple—because there is so much that it claims not to be. However, in fact, the Realization of the Truth of the *Ribhu Gita* requires—as a prerequisite to the "ultimate practice" it argues and represents, and, also, to the final fulfillment of that practice—the most intense penetration and transcending of the paradoxes of life, mind, and egoity. Throughout the text of chapter twenty-six—which is in the form of an address given to Nidagha by the Sage—Ribhu often repeats the admonition: "Abide As That". The clauses that follow the admonition are usually either descriptions of "That" or of what "That" is not. The question of exactly how to "Abide As That" is not elaborately indicated—but the text does speak aphoristically about some of the rudimentary fundamentals of the "how". Indeed, as the title of this presentation of chapter twenty-six suggests, the basic practice indicated by the Sage Ribhu is, simply: "Abide As That".

The Sage Ribhu recommends the classic remedy of the "Advaitic" tradition of Non-Dualism—the "only one formless undifferentiated Reality" school of Asian Indian philosophy and practice. Thus, it is said: You should think (or tacitly feel) that everything that is apparently known is "That" (the one, indivisible, formless, absolute, all-pervading Reality), and that you, also—because everything and everyone inheres in What is one, indivisible, and all-pervading—are That. When all ordinary thoughts have been purified and undermined by this tacitly felt one-thought—then, abandon or surrender or renounce even this (tacitly felt) one-thought. In that event, you will simply, spontaneously, and inherently Abide <u>As</u> That—or with the natural, spontaneous feeling of intrinsically self-evident identity with That.

The reader should understand that actual Realization of "That" requires more of one than a thought (or even a tacit feeling) of "That". The text of the *Ribhu Gita* represents that genre of transcendentalist literature in which What can be Awakened only in the ultimate course of a profound, unfathomable sacrifice of egoity is described almost offhand, in the simplest terms—with barely a metaphor's worth of symbol for the necessary ordeal of preliminaries.

If you would truly "Abide <u>As</u> That", then—as even <u>all</u> traditions have always declared—you must submit to become thus and so enabled.

ADI DA SAMRAJ
TAT SUNDARAM HERMITAGE
DECEMBER 7, 2005

2.

The Legendary Story of The Sage Ribhu and His Devotee Nidagha, As Told By Avatar Adi Da Samraj

Although the Sage Ribhu taught His devotee the Supreme Truth of the Absolute Reality as indivisibly one, and without a second, Nidagha, in spite of his education and training, did not get sufficient "self"-understanding and equanimity to adopt and follow the transcendental Way of intrinsic Self-knowledge. Thus, Nidagha settled down in his native town—to lead a rather conventional life, devoted to the observance of ceremonial religion.

The Sage Ribhu loved His devotee Nidagha deeply—just as the latter (in spite of his evident immaturity) truly loved and venerated his Master. In spite of his elderly age, Ribhu would, at times, require Himself to go to His devotee in the town—in order to see if the latter had yet outgrown his pious ritualism. At times, the Sage went to the town in disguise—so that He might observe how Nidagha would act when he did not know that he was being observed by his Master.

On one such occasion, Ribhu—who had put on the disguise of a peasant farmer—found Nidagha intently and enthusiastically watching an oncoming procession. Unrecognized by the towndweller (Nidagha), the "peasant farmer" (Ribhu) enquired what the excitement was all about—and was told, by Nidagha, that the "royal person" was "going in Procession"!

"Oh! it is the royal person! He goes in procession! And where exactly is <u>he</u>?" asked the "peasant farmer".

"There, on the elephant," said Nidagha.

"You say the royal person is on the elephant. Yes, I see the <u>two</u>," said the "peasant farmer"—"but which is the royal person and which is the elephant?"

"What!" exclaimed the offended Nidagha. "You see the two, but do not know that the man above is the royal person and the animal below is the elephant? Where is the use of talking to a stupid person like you?"

"Please, do not be too impatient with me—for I am only an ignorant man," begged the "peasant farmer". "You said 'above' and 'below'. What do <u>they</u> mean?"

Nidagha could tolerate the fool's enquiry no more. "You see the royal person and the elephant—the one evidently <u>above</u> and the other evidently <u>below</u>. Yet, you want to know what is <u>meant</u> by 'above' and 'below'?"—burst out Nidagha. "If things seen and words spoken convey so little meaning to you, action alone must teach you. Bend forward, old man, and you will know it immediately—and all <u>too</u> well!"

The "peasant farmer" did as he was told. Nidagha got onto his shoulders, and said, "Know it now. I am <u>above</u>, like the royal person—and you are <u>below</u>, like the elephant. Is that not clear enough?"

"No, not yet," was the "peasant farmer's" quiet reply. "You say <u>you</u> are <u>above</u>, like the royal person—and <u>I</u> am <u>below</u>, like the elephant. The 'royal person', the 'elephant', 'above', and 'below'—so far, all is clear. Please, tell me—what <u>exactly</u> do you <u>mean</u> by 'I' and 'you'?"

When Nidagha was thus confronted—all of a sudden!—with the mighty problem of defining the "you" apart from the "I", all presumed dualities and differences vanished from his mind. At once, Nidagha understood that the words "you" and "I" are merely conventions of spoken language, in exchanges between bodily-evident—but never otherwise defined—persons. It became suddenly self-evident to Nidagha that neither he, nor the "peasant farmer", nor any one ever or at all has ever known either an internal or an other separate "self" (or ego-"I") itself, apart from the bodily and conventionally apparent persons of daily speech.

Immediately, with this vanishing of the illusory mind of "difference", Nidagha jumped down from the shoulders of the "peasant farmer", and fell in sudden recognition at the feet of his <u>Master</u>, saying: "Who else but my Great Master, the Sage Ribhu, could have thus Awakened me, from the superficial mind of physical existence, to the indivisible State of Being that <u>Is</u> the true and inherently egoless Self? Oh! Benign Master, I crave your forgiveness and your forever continued Blessing-Grace!"

3.

The Essence of The Non-Dualist Reality-Teachings of
The Sage Ribhu

The ego-idea, "I-am-the-body", arises from the internal faculty of sensation—the mind. The ego-idea, "I-am-the-body", is the essence of the illusion of bondage. The root-idea of "self"-identification with the body is the essence of bondage to birth and death. The root-identification of fundamental Being (Itself) with the merely apparent body is the source of all fears. If there is not even a trace of the "I-am-the-body" idea—everything will be found to be the Indivisible Self-Reality of Intrinsically Self-Evident Being (Itself).

The ego-idea—"I-am-the-body"—is the root-ignorance. It is known as the primal knot, the origin of all bondage—the knot of the heart. That root-ignorance—the root-idea, the ego-idea, "I-am-the-body"—

gives rise (coincidently) to the idea of birth (or of conditional existence) and to the idea of death (or of eventual non-existence). If there is not even a trace of the "I-am-the-body" idea—everything will be found to be the Indivisible Self-Reality of Intrinsically Self-Evident Being (Itself).

The ego-"I" is a mere idea. "God", the world, the separate "self", all desires, all actions, all fear, all sorrow, all anger, and even all things are mere ideas.

Self-Abiding (or Merely Being)—without any ideas—Is the Indivisible State of no-difference. Fundamental Being Is (Itself) inherence in and As the Supreme Being. Merely to Be (As Is) Is (Itself) true knowledge. Self-Evident Being Is Itself Liberation. Merely to Be (As Is) Is (Itself) the Intrinsically Self-Evident, Real, True, and Transcendental State. Self-Evident Being Is (Itself) the Intrinsically Self-Evident Self-Reality That Is Reality Itself. Intrinsically Self-Evident Being Is (Itself) the Supreme Formless Reality otherwise thought and sought as "God". If there are no ideas at all—everything will be found to be the Indivisible Self-Reality of Intrinsically Self-Evident Being (Itself).

The body and the various internal functions (of sensation, mind, emotion, and breath) are mere ideas. Listening, thinking, and meditating are mere ideas. Enquiry (or even any method of seeking) into the Ultimate Nature of one's own existence is a mere idea. Any and every "thing" is a mere idea. Ideas give rise to the separate world, the separate "self", and the separate "God". There is nothing that appears or arises except mere ideas. Everything is, in Truth, the Indivisible Self-Reality of Intrinsically Self-Evident Being (Itself).

The apparently separate ego-mind of mere ideas is not, itself, the Indivisible Self-Reality. The apparently separate ego-mind of mere ideas is like a magic show of mere illusions. The ego-mind of ideas is like the son of a childless woman. The apparently separate ego-mind of mere ideas is inherently non-existent. There is no separately existing mind. Therefore, there are no separately existing ideas—and no separately existing "self" (or ego-"I"). All apparently arising ideas are only the Indivisible Self-Reality of Intrinsically Self-Evident Being (Itself).

4.

Abide As That
On The Practice of Self-Abiding As The Indivisible Self-
Reality of Intrinsically Self-Evident Being, Itself
Chapter twenty-six of the *Ribhu Gita*

1. Now, I will explain to you the practice of Self-Abiding As the Indivisible Self-Reality of Intrinsically Self-Evident Being (Itself). This teaching is of an esoteric and arcane nature—very difficult to understand rightly, even with the help of traditional Scriptures. Accomplished luminaries in other planes, and illustrious practitioners of Spiritual discipline here, and even those who staunchly uphold and argue the non-dual principles of this instruction are yet far from the actual Realization of the Truth of Intrinsically Self-Evident Being (Itself)—even after great efforts of renunciation, extraordinary exercises of virtue, and intense seeking for Liberation and Divine destiny. Therefore, be serious with me, As I Am—and, thus and carefully, examine all of my argument—and, merely (or only) by Self-Abiding As the Indivisible Self-Reality of Intrinsically Self-Evident Being (Itself), Be always Happy.

2. Truly Self-Realized Sages say that inherence in Reality means Self-Abiding As the inherently indivisible, non-dual, non-separate, non-different, non-conditional, egoless, and actionless Absolute Supreme Being—Which is Self-Existing As Consciousness (Itself), Self-Radiant As Bliss (Itself), and universally Self-Evident As the true and very Self (or inherent Mere Being) of all. Therefore, the method universally taught by all truly Self-Realized Sages is that of dissolving the mind in Intrinsically Self-Evident Being (Itself)—like milk is dissolved in water—and, thus, to Self-Abide, inherently free of all thinking.

3. If whatever is apparently arising as experience is directly examined, it is readily obvious that everything apparently arising as experience is without independent existence, and without "substance" or "identity" in and of itself—but everything is only of the one and Indivisible Self-Nature (or Self-Reality) of Intrinsically Self-Evident Being (Itself), Which is not different from the Self-Evidence of Mere Being that is one's own true and very Self-Condition. Allow the Intrinsically Self-Evident knowledge of Mere Being (or of your own true and very Self-Condition) to become firmly established in you, by means of constant practice. Then—when Intrinsic knowledge of Mere Being is stably firm in you—renounce all ideas, and Merely Self-Abide As the Indivisible Self-Reality of Intrinsically Self-Evident Being (Itself). Thus—merely by Self-Abiding As the Indivisible Self-Reality of Intrinsically Self-Evident Being (Itself)—Be always Happy.

4. Abide As That Which does not, upon direct examination, exhibit any signs of duality, division, difference, or separateness—or even any of the cause-and-effect characteristics of conditionality. Abide As That in Which—when the mind is dissolved in It—there is no fear, or any anxious anticipation of differences at all. Abide As That, and, thus, Be always Happy, and fearless, and free from all the implications of the seeming of duality.

5. Abide As That in Which there are neither ideas nor visions, neither passivity nor anxious "self"-control, neither mental reflections of the world nor exercises of intellectual effort, neither doubt nor certainty, neither conditionally existing being nor apparent non-existence of being, and no perception of opposites and differences at all. Merely Abide As That, and, thus, Be always Happy, and fearless, and free from all the implications of the seeming of duality.

6. Abide <u>As</u> That in Which there is neither any negative characteristic nor any positive quality, neither pleasure nor pain, neither active thinking nor a strategically made-silent mind, neither suffering nor any austerities of seeking to escape from suffering—and no identification with the body as "self", nor any identification with any "objects" at all. Merely Abide <u>As</u> That, and, thus, <u>Be</u> always Happy, free from any and every kind of idea or thought.

7. Abide <u>As</u> That in Which there is no effort of seeking—whether physical, mental, verbal, or of any other kind—and neither any addictions of desire, nor any "self"-satisfaction with good works, nor any attachments at all, and not even any results of any actions of desire. Merely Abide <u>As</u> That, and, thus, <u>Be</u> always Happy, free from any and every kind of idea or thought.

8. Abide <u>As</u> That in Which there are neither thoughts nor a would-be thinker there—and neither the apparent arising, nor the apparent support and continuation, nor the apparent destruction or ending of any thing or any world. Abide <u>As</u> That in Which there is no thing or world in space or time. Merely Abide <u>As</u> That, and, thus, <u>Be</u> always Happy, free from any and every kind of idea or thought.

9. Abide <u>As</u> That in Which there are neither any illusions nor any of their "self"-deluding power or effect, neither any conditional knowledge nor any absence of right knowledge, neither separate "self" nor separate "Creator-God", neither any conditionally apparent "is" nor any conditionally apparent "is not", neither any conditional world nor any condition-imposing "God". Merely Abide <u>As</u> That, and, thus, <u>Be</u> always Happy, free from any and every kind of idea or thought.

10. Abide <u>As</u> That in Which there is no separate Deity (or "Creator-God", or Divine "Other"), nor worship of any one or many "gods" and "goddesses" of any kinds at all, and no multiple "Divine Aspects",

nor any meditation on Deity, or Aspect, or Divine Modes of Divine Doings, and no "Formless God" either, nor any meditation on any thought of a "Formless One". Merely Abide <u>As</u> That, and, thus, <u>Be</u> always Happy, free from any and every kind of idea or thought.

11. Abide <u>As</u> That in Which there is neither bondage to the "method" of good works nor devotional search toward the "Divine Being" nor any conceit of book-learning and presumptions of superiority in mind—and no goal or result of any kind of seeking-effort to be attained, and no separate inwardness of "Supreme State" to be swooned about, and, indeed, not any "object" of any kind to be acquired or achieved by any means at all. Merely Abide <u>As</u> That, and, thus, <u>Be</u> always Happy, free from any and every kind of idea or thought.

12. Abide <u>As</u> That in Which there is neither body nor faculties of sensation nor any circulation of vital energies or forces, neither concepts nor calculations nor fantasies, neither separate ego-"I" nor illusions of any kind, nor any kind of inwardness or "point of view" that either supports or identifies with any mode of separateness or difference at all—and not even any kind of "macrocosm" or "microcosm" anywhere. Merely Abide <u>As</u> That, and, thus, <u>Be</u> always Happy, free from any and every kind of idea or thought.

13. Abide <u>As</u> That in Which there is neither desire nor anger at its frustration, neither greed nor delusion by its satisfaction, neither reactive negativity nor contempt nor lack of sympathy nor pride of "self"-image—and, altogether, no mental impurity, no presumption of inherent bondage, and no counter-presumption of a Liberated "self". Merely Abide <u>As</u> That, and, thus, <u>Be</u> always Happy, free from any and every kind of idea or thought.

14. Abide <u>As</u> That in Which there is neither beginning nor end, neither "above" nor "below" nor any "in-between", no temple and no

priest, no sacred offerings, no pious deeds—and, indeed, no time, no space, and no perceptual "objects" anywhere. Merely Abide <u>As</u> That, and, thus, <u>Be</u> always Happy, free from any and every kind of idea or thought.

15. Abide <u>As</u> That in Which there are no opposites in opposition anywhere, no "yes" or any "no", no desireless separate "self", no "virtuous character", no search for Liberation, no separation between Master and devotee, no acquired Realization, no advanced state of achievement, no conditional state of Liberation, here or after death—and, indeed, not any "thing" whatsoever or at any time. Merely Abide <u>As</u> That, and, thus, <u>Be</u> always Happy, free from any and every kind of idea or thought.

16. Abide <u>As</u> That in Which there are no "Holy Books", no "talking schools", no orthodoxies to be argued, no objections, no counter-arguments, no theories about anything or everything, no assertions, no denials—and, indeed, no "anything" at all that seems to have an existence independent of the inherently egoless Self of Mere Being, always already prior to mind and argument. Merely Abide <u>As</u> That, and, thus, <u>Be</u> always Happy, free from any and every kind of idea or thought.

17. Abide <u>As</u> That in Which no "pros" and "cons" compete, no winning or losing is at stake, no words arise to "mean", no speech is made of utterance, no differences pertain, no separation between the "self" and the "Supreme Being" is defined—and, indeed, neither cause nor effect is discernible at all. Merely Abide <u>As</u> That, and, thus, <u>Be</u> always Happy, free from any and every kind of idea or thought.

18. Abide <u>As</u> That in Which there is no need for listening, pondering, and contemplating, no prescript of meditation (or any meditative concentration of attention) to be engaged for any purpose,

no logical distinctions to be made between sameness, otherness, or contradictoriness—and, indeed, no definitions of meanings arise to make distinctions of any kind. Merely Abide <u>As</u> That, and, thus, <u>Be</u> always Happy, free from any and every kind of idea or thought.

19. Abide <u>As</u> That in Which there are no fears of an anticipated hell, no joys of an anticipated heaven, no worlds made by the "Creator-God" or any other "gods" and "goddesses" at all, nor any "objects" to be acquired from "higher powers" by tricks and prayers, no "other worlds" of any kind—and, indeed, not even any cosmic universe at all. Merely Abide <u>As</u> That, and, thus, <u>Be</u> always Happy, free from any and every kind of idea or thought.

20. Abide <u>As</u> That in Which there are no constituent elements, nor even an atom or a molecule of elementally constituted anything, nor any "point of view" or ego-"I" or ego-mind or ego's thoughts and fantasies, no jot of blemish, stain, or dust—and, indeed, not even the first concept yet. Merely Abide <u>As</u> That, and, thus, <u>Be</u> always Happy, free from any and every kind of idea or thought.

21. Abide <u>As</u> That in Which there are neither gross nor subtle nor causal bodies of any kind or number, nor any conditional states of conditional being, no waking, no dreaming, and no deep sleep, no different degrees of "advancement of soul", no bodily afflictions, no natural disasters, no threats from "entities" in the deeps of things, no functionally differentiated faculties of body-mind—and, indeed, no separate-"self"-illusion to identify with faculties and forms and events. Merely Abide <u>As</u> That, and, thus, <u>Be</u> always Happy, free from any and every kind of idea or thought.

22. Abide <u>As</u> That in Which there are no "objects" of psycho-physical perception, no powers that can delude or hide or fool or cheat, no apprehension of any kind of difference, no un-Reality, no "powers"

of any kind—and, indeed, no falsity, or even any absence of lucidity. Merely Abide <u>As</u> That, and, thus, <u>Be</u> always Happy, free from any and every kind of idea or thought.

23. Abide <u>As</u> That in Which there are no sense-organs, and no one to exercise them—That in Which Self-Existing and Self-Radiant Bliss is Self-Evident, That Which is Itself always already Self-Evident, That Which, when Self-Realized, is Self-Evidently deathless, and, indeed, That in and of Which neither birth nor life nor death is Real or true. Merely Abide <u>As</u> That, and, thus, <u>Be</u> always Happy, free from any and every kind of idea or thought.

24. Abide <u>As</u> That Which, when Self-Realized, inherently Self-Reveals all conditional happiness to be a mere reflection of Its own inherent Bliss, and That Which, when Self-Realized, inherently Self-Reveals there is no "other" of any kind—and, indeed, That Which, when Self-Realized, inherently Self-Reveals there is no separate any one at all. Merely Abide <u>As</u> That, and, thus, <u>Be</u> always Happy, free from any and every kind of idea or thought.

25. Abide <u>As</u> That Which, when Self-Realized <u>As</u> one's true and very Self, inherently Self-Reveals there is not anything else or other to be known—and, indeed, that all the What that <u>Is</u> is always already known, and every necessary purpose has always already been accomplished. Merely Abide <u>As</u> That, and, thus, <u>Be</u> always Happy, free from any and every kind of idea or thought.

26. Abide <u>As</u> That Which is immediately Self-Realized (<u>As</u> one's true and very Self) when non-difference from the Indivisible Self-Condition of Reality Itself is Self-Apprehended to <u>Be</u> Self-Evident, That Which, when Self-Realized <u>As</u> Itself, inherently Self-Reveals Reality Itself to <u>Be</u> Self-Evident <u>and</u> Self-Radiant, <u>As</u> Bliss Itself—and, indeed, That Which, when the mind is dissolved in It, inherently

Self-Reveals Itself to Be inherently and entirely satisfactory. Merely Abide As That, and, thus, Be always Happy, free from any and every kind of idea or thought.

27. Abide As That in Which, when the mind is dissolved in It, all suffering immediately ceases, and the idea of a separate "I", or of any separate "you", or of any separate "other", or of even any experience of relatedness at all is inherently vanished—and, indeed, even all conception and perception of difference is utterly gone away. Merely Abide As That, and, thus, Be always Happy, free from any and every kind of idea or thought.

28. Abide As That in Which, when the mind is dissolved in It, only one remains, without a second, and nothing other than Mere Being (Itself) is known to be—and, indeed, only Bliss is Evident, and, altogether, Self-Evidently so. Merely Abide As That, and, thus, Be always Happy, free from any and every kind of idea or thought.

29. Abide As That Which is Indivisible Self-Existence (Itself), Indivisible Consciousness (Itself), and Indivisible Bliss (Itself), utterly without duality, but inherently and entirely non-separate, non-different, non-dual, one, indivisible, and absolute. Merely by tacitly knowing you Are That, Be always Happy.

30. Abide As That Which Is one, all, only, and perfect. Merely by tacitly knowing you Are That, Be always Happy.

31. Abide As That in Which there is no mind, no thoughts, no ideas of any kind, no sense-perceptions, no things, no others, no "point of view", no ego-"I", no desires, and no confusions or contradictions of any kind. Merely by tacitly knowing you Are That, Be always Happy.

32. Abide <u>As</u> That in Which there is no awareness of the body, no participation in the faculties of body and mind, no perception of "objects", and no conception of "objects" of <u>any</u> kind—That in Which the mind is inactive and non-existent, and the tacit awareness of Merely <u>Being</u> is directly apprehended to be non-different from Indivisible Reality Itself. Merely by tacitly knowing you <u>Are</u> That, <u>Be</u> always Happy.

33. Abide <u>As</u> That in Which there is no longer any purpose to be achieved by meditation, because meditative concentration of attention is not useful as a means for tacit knowledge of Reality to be directly Self-Realized—That in Which no presumption of ignorance, or of acquired and conditional knowledge, or of any motivation toward activity of any kind arises, because It <u>Is</u> the one and Indivisible Reality Itself. Merely by tacitly knowing you <u>Are</u> That, <u>Be</u> always Happy.

34. Abide <u>As</u> That in Which no seeming difference can make a difference in Its State, and, therefore, <u>only</u> Bliss <u>Is</u>—and there is <u>no</u> suffering, and <u>no</u> "objects" are known at all, and <u>no</u> activity or process or event is experienced or followed, and <u>no</u> thought of separate "self" arises, but only the one and Indivisible Reality <u>Is</u>. Merely by tacitly knowing you <u>Are</u> That, <u>Be</u> always Happy.

35. Abide <u>As</u> That Which <u>Is</u> one and only—the Indivisible, Transcendental, Formless Reality, the Intrinsically Self-Evident Self-Reality, the absolute and perfect State of Being, Consciousness <u>Itself</u>, the Supreme Truth. Merely by tacitly knowing you <u>Are</u> That, <u>Be</u> always Happy.

36. Abide <u>As</u> That Which <u>Is</u> Self-Evident Self-Existing Being, Self-Radiant <u>As</u> Bliss, inherently non-dual, indivisible, and only one. Merely by tacitly knowing you <u>Are</u> That, <u>Be</u> always Happy.

37. Abide <u>As</u> That Which <u>Is</u> Truth, Peace, Existence Itself, Self-Existing Being (Itself), without form, or accessory, or divisible attributes, or conditional characteristics—the one and only and inherently perfect Being, the inherently egoless Self-Condition of all. Merely by tacitly knowing you <u>Are</u> That, <u>Be</u> always Happy.

38. Abide <u>As</u> That Which Is everything (from the conditional "point of view") and nothing (from the Absolute Position of no "point of view" at all)—Self-Existing <u>As</u> Mere Being (Itself), Self-Evident <u>As</u> Consciousness (Itself), Self-Radiant <u>As</u> Bliss (Itself), inherently actionless and at rest, Merely Being That from Which there is no separation. Merely by tacitly knowing you <u>Are</u> That, <u>Be</u> always Happy.

39. Now, I have explained to you the practice of Self-Abiding <u>As</u> the Indivisible Self-Reality of Intrinsically Self-Evident Being (Itself). By constantly thinking (or tacitly feeling) that you <u>Are</u> the Indivisible Self-Reality of Intrinsically Self-Evident Being (Itself), you can attain the State of always Self-Abiding <u>As</u> That—and, thus and so, Self-Realize inherent Bliss. When, by means of such constant thinking (or the constant exercise of such tacit feeling), you <u>Are</u> Merely Self-Abiding <u>As</u> the Indivisible Self-Reality of Intrinsically Self-Evident Being (Itself), you <u>Are</u> inherently and truly Self-Established <u>As</u> That—then (and thereafter) you <u>Are</u> inherently free of all identification with birth, life, suffering, and death.

40. "<u>Everything</u> that (apparently) arises is <u>only</u> the Supreme Being—Self-Existing <u>As</u> Mere Being (Itself), Self-Evident <u>As</u> Consciousness (Itself), and Self-Radiant <u>As</u> Bliss (Itself)—and I <u>Am</u> That." Renounce, relinquish, and remove all limited and ego-binding thoughts—by constantly resorting to the affirmation (or tacit intending) of <u>this</u> one Great Thought (or Feeling-Attitude). At last—when this <u>one</u> Great Thought (or tacit Feeling-Attitude)

is stabilized, and all other thoughts (and feelings) are removed (or inherently transcended) by Its means—surrender (or renounce and abandon) even this one Great Thought (or tacitly-intended Feeling-Attitude), and (<u>thus</u>) Merely Self-Abide <u>As</u> the Indivisible Self-Reality of Intrinsically Self-Evident Being (Itself), or That Which was Indicated by the one tacitly-intended Great Thought (or Great Feeling-Attitude). In This Manner, Self-Realize and <u>Be</u> the non-dual, Indivisible Supreme Being—and, <u>thus</u>, <u>Be</u> Liberation <u>Itself</u>.

41. The oppositions of positive and negative thoughts are a constant and inevitable characteristic of the sense-based mind. There are <u>no</u> thoughts of any kind in the Self-Evident State (and Indivisible Self-Reality) of Supreme Being. Therefore, Merely Self-Abide, <u>As</u> That, inherently free from any and every kind of idea or thought—even like a stone or a log of wood. Thus and inherently free of mind, you <u>Are</u> That Which <u>Is</u> (inherently and always) Happiness <u>Itself</u>.

42. By constantly resorting to the one Great Thought (or tacitly-intended Feeling-Attitude), of inherent Self-Identification with the Indivisible Self-Reality of Intrinsically Self-Evident Being (Itself), and (thus and thereby) forgetting (or priorly transcending) all other thoughts—and (at last) by surrendering (or renouncing and abandoning) even That one tacitly-intended Great Thought (or Great Feeling-Attitude), and (thus and then) Self-Abiding <u>As</u> the Indivisible Self-Reality of Intrinsically Self-Evident Being (Itself)— you will Realize and Merely <u>Be</u> the non-separate and all-inclusive Supreme Being (<u>Itself</u>). Even a great sinner, who listens to this teaching with right understanding, and truly practices its discipline, will (by means of Blessing-Grace and all of right practice) be relieved of the burden and the seeking-effort of all sinning—and even such a one will, in due course, Realize and <u>Be</u> the one and Indivisible Supreme Being.

43. The traditions contain an endless stream of practice-texts and means
and paths of Spiritual instruction, well-describing the various disciplines and meditations prescribed for the necessary purification of
body and mind—and which <u>must</u> precede the practice I have now
explained to you. Therefore, I have here explained <u>only</u> the ultimate
practice, and the Ultimate State, of Self-Abiding <u>As</u> the Indivisible
Self-Reality of Intrinsically Self-Evident Being (Itself)—in order
that those who, by means of the right exercise of all the necessary
preliminary methods (of meditation, self-discipline, and the like),
have become purified in body and mind may <u>Be</u> Liberated, by Self-
Realizing inherent Bliss, inherently free of mind (and, like stone,
inherently free from any and every kind of idea or thought), and <u>so</u>
Merely Self-Abide <u>As</u> the indivisible, non-separate, and all-inclusive
Supreme Formless Divine State of Being.

44. Effectively practicing renunciation of the mind (and all ideas and
thoughts), by constantly thinking (or tacitly intending) the one
Great Thought (or Great Feeling-Attitude)—that <u>everything
known</u> is <u>only</u> the one and indivisible Supreme Being, and <u>That</u>
one and indivisible Supreme Being <u>Is</u> oneself—and, thereafter, having surrendered (or inherently transcended) even the tacit intending of That one Great Thought (or Great Feeling-Attitude), by
Self-Abiding <u>As</u> the State of inherent Self-Identification with the
Intrinsically Self-Evident State of Supreme Being, Liberation can
be Self-Realized, in the here and now. <u>Thus</u>, I have spoken the
Truth.

45. When one has directly established that one <u>Is</u> (always) That Which
<u>Is</u> Self-Existing, Self-Evident, Self-Radiant, one, indivisible, and
non-separate—and when, on that basis, one <u>Is</u> merely (or always
already) Self-Abiding <u>As</u> That, inherently free from any and every
kind of idea or thought—then, all un-Reality is finally transcended,
and all merely seeming bondage to identification with body, mind,

birth, life, suffering, and death is entirely vanished, and Liberation (Itself) is truly Self-Realized.

The Indivisible Self-Reality of Intrinsically Self-Evident Being (Itself) <u>Is</u> the true and esoteric Significance of the "God"-Symbol of all religions—Dancing above all and everything, one and only, Supreme, and in the Self-Intoxicated Mood of inherent Bliss.

<u>Thus</u>, the Sage Ribhu expounded the inherently Free State of Mere Being to His gratefully Blessed devotee, Nidagha.

XII

SIXTH-STAGE METHOD VERSUS PERFECT PRACTICE

✣

A Discourse Given by Avatar Adi Da Samraj to
His devotees, on December 11, 2005—directly after He
had first Recited His Rendering of the Ribhu Gita

There is a clear sympathy between the only-by-Me Revealed and Given Reality-Way of Adidam and the traditional Non-dualist Teachings. Nevertheless, the Reality-Way of Adidam is not merely a re-statement or a re-presentation of the traditional Non-dualist Teachings. The Reality-Way of Adidam is a new Revelation That Completes the Great Tradition as a whole—and Completes, then, the sixth stage tradition of the Sages.

What is there in the text of the *Ribhu Gita* that may be said to be (in some sense) different from—or (in some manner, or to some degree) of a lesser nature (or less developed) than—the "Perfect Practice" of the Reality-Way of Adidam?

In the *Ribhu Gita*, the Sage Ribhu says, over and over again, "Abide As That, Abide As That, Abide As That"—and He then describes what Reality is not, or He describes something of Its Characteristics over against descriptions of what It is not. What Ribhu says is an admonition to practice—"Abide As That Which Is of such-and-such a Nature, That Which Is not such-and-such, That Which Is not (in any sense) a thought or a form of thinking or a characteristic of the mind. Abide As That. Now you have been instructed. Be happy."

162

On the face of it, Ribhu's instruction sounds like what might even be called a "shortcut" to Ultimate Truth, and you are simply being told it: "Now you <u>Are</u> That, so <u>Be</u> Happy—<u>Thus</u>." However—now that you have listened to this admonition—why are <u>you</u> not (<u>Thus</u>) Happy? If someone wants to argue that he or she <u>is</u> (<u>Thus</u>) Happy—then I could, of course, Address that person. However, since it appears evident that, having listened to this admonition, you have not Realized what the admonition calls you to Realize, then you are not Abiding <u>As</u> That.

This fact points out what one might suppose (in fact) to be a limitation in this text. The Realization that is indicated in the *Ribhu Gita* is not effectively Established by philosophical argumentation—nor <u>can</u> It be effectively Established by philosophical argumentation. If such philosophizing were sufficient, then to listen to a recitation of this text would be sufficient for Realization.

If simply listening to the communication of the *Ribhu Gita* were sufficient to establish the Realization described therein, then anyone who reads or listens to the text would be immediately Established in That Realization. However, philosophical argumentation <u>cannot</u> "cause" Transcendental or (otherwise) Divine Self-Realization. Traditional texts often seem to speak as if philosophical argumentation could establish the Realization of Truth—but, in actuality, it cannot.

At the end of chapter twenty-six of the *Ribhu Gita,* several verses speak rather "programatically" about what to do. A practice is described that amounts to the overwhelming (and, thus, the replacing) of all thoughts, all concepts, all ideas, and all activities of mind, by the persistent introduction (or re-introduction) of a primal thought, a principal thought, a <u>thought</u> that (somehow) eliminates <u>thought</u>. Even the word "thought" does not quite encompass the instruction, as people commonly understand the word "thought" to mean (as a kind of verbal process).

Therefore, in Rendering this text, I have introduced an alternative phrasing: "tacitly-intended Feeling-Attitude of inherent Self-Identification with the Indivisible Self-Reality of Intrinsically

Self-Evident Being (Itself)". The practice described in the *Ribhu Gita* is the constant re-asserting of this feeling-attitude (or feeling-presumption, or "one thought"), until the State of Self-Abiding <u>As</u> That Which is represented by such "thought" (or feeling-intention) Is Established. When the practitioner is effectively Abiding <u>As</u> That, then there is no longer any requirement for any kind of practice in the form of a feeling-intention (or feeling-assertion, or one-pointed thought).

Thus, there is a practice of maintaining an affirmation, <u>without</u> conceptual thought, and (yet) intended, asserted, felt, or (in some manner or other) "thought" (so to speak)—and this practice would, according to this text, result in Transcendental Self-Abiding, or the State of "Abiding <u>As</u> That", which is the fundamental admonition that is repeated in the text.

Is the presumption true? Is there, in fact, any kind of thought (or tacit feeling) that can establish Transcendental Self-Abiding? There are many forms of practice recommended in the Great Tradition altogether—and many forms of practice are recommended in the sixth stage tradition (or the tradition of the Sages, or the Non-dualist Teachers) in particular. All of the variant kinds of sixth stage practice could (fundamentally) be said to be, in one form or another, variants on the practice described by Ribhu.

The Teaching of the *Ribhu Gita* is a kind of epitome of the "method" of the Sages. Ramana Maharshi, for example, was a Teacher in the mode of the sixth stage Non-dualist tradition. Ramana Maharshi's recommendation was essentially to hold to the "I"-thought (or the "I"-feeling), until you become established in the Source of that—or, that is to say, until you become established <u>As</u> the Transcendental "Self". Then that practice is no longer necessary, because Self-Abiding follows.

Thus, Ramana Maharshi's Teaching is, essentially, a variant form of the Teaching of Ribhu. Others recommend using the "Mahavakyas", the "Great Utterances" from the Upanishads—"I am Brahman", "Thou Art That", and so on. As such, the "Mahavakyas" are verbal formulas to be "considered", to be felt, to be tacitly asserted—even, at first, to be thought, but, then (beyond thought), to be felt as a tacit affirmation ("considering" the Utterance to the point of deepest potential contemplation of the Truth of it), ultimately leading to Transcendental Self-Identification (or Abiding <u>As</u> That).

Fundamentally, the entire sixth stage tradition of the Sages (or the Non-dualist tradition) involves this kind of practice—this "one thought" (or tacit feeling) that is presumed to become Transcendental Self-Abiding. There are non-"Advaitic" (but, nevertheless, ultimately, Non-dualist) variations on the sixth stage tradition, especially in the schools of Buddhism (and, also, but more secondarily, in the schools of Jainism, of Taoism, and, even more anciently, of the Samkhya tradition). The sixth stage variation represented by the earliest (or so-called "Hinayana") tradition of Buddhism approaches the practice in a somewhat different manner than that of traditional Advaitism, by means of an effort to stand beyond what is "not-self" (or "no-self"). That procedure involves the direct observing of conditionally arising phenomena (especially the phenomena associated with the psycho-physical events of functional perception within the body-mind-complex itself), and (thus and thereby) noting (in detail) the contents and characteristics of the arising phenomena, and understanding all of that (<u>thus</u>, and <u>as</u> mere conditionality, inherently "not-self", or only "no-self"), and (in this manner) establishing an attitude of mere observing (or detachment) relative to all thus observed phenomena—until only That Which Is Always Already "The Case" is Self-Established (or "left over", or Realized to <u>Be</u> Always Already Self-Established <u>As</u> "The Case"). In any case, this approach (and even any other "method" of detachment, leading toward Transcendental Realization) is, inherently and inevitably, always founded on the one and only and fundamental sixth stage basis.

In the Advaitic tradition, the Divine Reality is pointed at through words—but in many schools of Buddhism, the Divine Reality is, as a general (but not absolute) rule, not described at all (or given any words of reference). In the schools of Buddhism, there are formulas for application of the mind—the use of koans, for instance, and various other kinds of often-recited formulas or visualized prescriptive meditations. All kinds of such meditations and practices (associated with the fourth, the fifth, and the sixth stages of life) are found in the Great Tradition of humankind—and the tradition of such practices is referred to in the *Ribhu Gita*.

Likewise, there is an indication in the *Ribhu Gita* that this Transcendentalist Reality-Teaching, if it is to be rightly and effectively practiced, requires a foundation of preparedness that is established by various forms of "self"-discipline. Only those who are rightly prepared (or purified in body and mind) are presumed to be capable of engaging the traditional Transcendentalist Reality-Teaching. Thus, there are not only certain formulas for the "one-thought" (or tacit-feeling) approach in the sixth stage tradition, but there are also necessary preliminaries (or modes of practice) that must precede the Transcendentalist practice, which must be engaged until there is sufficient equanimity of body and mind (relative to action and thinking, and so on) to allow a pure Transcendentalist approach to be effective.

However, even after the preliminary practices are fulfilled, the Transcendentalist practice still begins (in the schools of Advaitism) with verbal formulas, or tacit feeling-affirmations (or tacit intentions of identification), of one kind or another—or (otherwise) with the variant modes of such practice found in the Buddhist tradition (as well as the traditions of Samkhya, Jainism, and, to a lesser extent, Taoism). Nevertheless, is it, in fact, true that Transcendental Self-Realization (or Transcendental Self-Abiding) can be Established by this "method" of "one-thought", or (in fact) by any conditional "method" whatsoever?

The verses of the *Ribhu Gita* that precede the admonitions on the "one-thought" practice give descriptions of the Transcendental Realization which are fundamentally compatible with My Own Descriptions of the first two stages of the "Perfect Practice" of the Reality-Way of Adidam—but what about Ribhu's descriptions of the "method" of Transcendental Realization? The "method" of philosophical argumentation is not, in fact, sufficient. If it were sufficient, then clear instruction would enable anyone who would simply listen to it intelligently to be (immediately) Transcendentally Self-Realized. And, indeed, it is traditionally said that one who reads or recites the *Ribhu Gita* over and over again will attain Self-Realization.

Many things are said in the Great Tradition—but simply because something is said does not mean that it is true. Ramana Maharshi was one of those who (from time to time) repeated the traditional statement that it would be sufficient to read chapter twenty-six of the *Ribhu Gita* or hear it recited. In fact, chapter twenty-six of the *Ribhu Gita* was often recited at Ramana Maharshi's Ashram during His lifetime.

Philosophical argumentation is not sufficient to Establish the Transcendental State of the Realization of Self-Evident Reality (Itself), and neither is "one-thought" (or any tacit feeling) enough. In fact, there is <u>no</u> form of psycho-physical practice that is enough (in and of itself) for any ultimate degree of Real-God-Realization.

The "Perfect Practice" of the only-by-Me Revealed and Given Reality-Way of Adidam has a unique characteristic that stands in contrast to the sixth stage tradition of the Sages. That unique characteristic is that the "Perfect Practice" of the Reality-Way of Adidam—or the practice of the Reality-Way of Adidam that is based on <u>Prior</u> Establishment of Transcendental Self-Realization—is Established not by philosophical argumentation, nor by "methods" of seeking via psycho-physical practices of one kind or another, but by <u>Transcendental Spiritual</u> Means— the Means of My Own Divine Avataric Transcendental Spiritual Self-Transmission. My Transcendental Spiritual Self-Transmission is not merely a conditional Spiritual Influence that stimulates deeper psycho-physical functioning (or psycho-physical Yogic processes) in the body-mind-complex. Nor is My Transcendental Spiritual Self-Transmission merely something in the realm of conditional existence that stimulates the body-mind-"self" toward some state of Transcendental Self-Realization—because, in that case, Transcendental Self-Realization would be dependent on conditional happenings and conditional changes, conditional functions of the body-mind-complex, and so on. Rather, the

Transcendental Spiritual Transmission That is Self-Manifested by Me in the Blessing of My devotees Is (Itself) the Transcendental, Inherently Spiritual, Intrinsically egoless, and Self-Evidently Divine Self-Nature, Self-Condition, and Self-State (Itself).

Consciousness Itself (or Self-Existing Being) is Self-Radiant, As the Indivisible Current of Love-Bliss-"Brightness". Such is the Inherent (or Intrinsic) Nature, Condition, and State of conditionally manifested reality. That Divine Transcendental Spiritual Force (or Current, or Presence) must be Self-Transmitted—directly Given, by Means of My Transcendentally Spiritually Self-Evident Blessing-Grace—and must (Thus and Thereby) Awaken My devotees to the Intrinsic Self-Apprehension of Self-Existing and Self-Radiant Being (Itself).

Thus, the only-by-Me Revealed and Given Reality-Way of Adidam is the Way in Which, by most profound (ego-surrendering, ego-forgetting, and ego-transcending) devotional means, My devotee is entered into devotional Communion with Me and is (most ultimately) Awakened, by My Direct Transcendental Spiritual Blessing-Transmission, to the Very Nature and Condition That Is My Intrinsically egoless and Self-Evidently Divine State. My Divine Avataric Transcendental Spiritual Self-Transmission, then, is not merely of a conditional nature, or merely a "cause" of conditional states.

My devotee may, of course, "experience" conditional states—even in the midst of being Immersed in My Blessing-Transmission. Yet, the True Transcendental Spiritual Process of the Reality-Way of Adidam is My Divine Avataric Transcendental Spiritual Self-Transmission of the Divine Self-Nature, Self-Condition, and Self-State Itself—Blessing and Awakening every one and all. My Divine Avataric Transcendental Spiritual Self-Transmission Is That to Which My devotee must be Awakened.

Therefore, the "Perfect Practice" of the only-by-Me Revealed and Given Reality-Way of Adidam is Established by Transcendental Spiritual Means—in the case of My devotees, or those who are whole bodily turned to Me, who are (thereby) entered into devotional Communion with Me, and who are obedient to My Instructions (such that the necessary discipline of the body-mind-complex is introduced into the life). Nevertheless, the Fundamental Process is the Direct Transcendental Spiritual Self-Transmission, by Me, of the Self-Existing and Self-Radiant Transcendental, Inherently Spiritual, Intrinsically egoless, and Self-Evidently Divine Self-Nature, Self-Condition, and Self-State.

My Divine Avataric Blessing-Transmission is a <u>Transcendental Spiritual</u> Transmission. It is the Transmission of That Which <u>Is</u> the Divine Self-Nature, Self-Condition, and Self-State. The Divine Self-Nature, Self-Condition, and Self-State is Transcendental <u>and</u> Inherently Spiritual. It <u>Is</u> the Love-Bliss-Full Current in and <u>As</u> Which everything and everyone is arising. It <u>Is</u> the Divine "Self" (or the True and Very and Intrinsically egoless Self-Nature, Self-Condition, and Self-State).

Thus, Consciousness Itself is not merely the detached awareness that notices "objects". Rather, Consciousness Itself Is the Very Self-Nature, Self-Condition, and Self-State of every apparent "self" and all apparent "objects". The Divine Self-Nature, Self-Condition, and Self-State Is the One and Indivisible Divine Conscious Light, Self-Existing and Self-Radiant.

The "Perfect Practice" of the only-by-Me Revealed and Given Reality-Way of Adidam is Established by this Divine Avataric Transcendental Spiritual Means—not by philosophical means, not by efforts of psycho-physical practice, and not by conditional achievement or seeking or conditional happenings, or by establishing conditions that (in and of themselves) are regarded to be Realization. Therefore, it is not possible to study My Reality-Teaching and come to Divine Self-Realization on that basis alone. My Reality-Teaching is simply an aspect of My Divine Avataric Transmission-Work. My Reality-Teaching only Serves to Clarify matters that need to be rightly understood by My devotees.

On the other hand, I Transmit Myself just as Directly to My dogs, or to the walls, as I do to My devotees. I was Speaking to one of the dogs the other day, and somebody was wondering what the difference is between humans and non-humans. I Said, "When you are not thinking, that is this dog."

There is no difference between the True (Divine) Self-Nature, Self-Condition, and Self-State of non-humans and of humans. Apparent functions can be pointed to that can be said to be different, but there is no fundamental difference. When you are not thinking, you are no different from a grasshopper or a blade of grass or a tree or My dogs. You are the same. You are in the same State. It is not merely that non-humans are like human beings, or that some non-humans are especially like human beings. The fact is that everything—all beings, every one and every thing altogether—is arising as an apparent modification of the One and Same Divine Self-Nature, Self-Condition, and Self-State (or Transcendental Spiritual Conscious Light). Thus, there is not, in Reality, the slightest difference between a human being, a dog, a tree, and a wall—not the slightest. There is not the slightest difference between you and the space in which you are apparently sitting. There is, in fact, no "difference" of any kind. There is no "difference". It is not that "difference" needs to be removed. "Difference" is not. "Difference" is something being superimposed by you.

That is what ego does. Because the activity that is egoity is happening, Transcendental Spiritual Divine Self-Realization cannot be Established merely by argument or by prescriptions of "self"-applied techniques, "methods", behaviors, beliefs, states of mind, states of body. Divine Self-Realization cannot be achieved by any means that is of a conditional nature.

That Which Is, Is—and It Transmits Itself. It is Self-Revealed. I Am the Self-Realization and the Self-Revelation of the Transcendental, Inherently Spiritual, Intrinsically egoless, and Self-Evidently Divine Self-Nature, Self-Condition, and Self-State—the "Bright", the Conscious Light—Avatarically Self-Manifested and Avatarically Self-Transmitted. I Am the Divine Avataric Means of your Realization—and this Means is directly Given. It is not conditionally made. It does not Awaken My devotees by establishing conditional states in My devotees. Rather,

My devotees are Awakened to My Avatarically Self-Revealed and Self-Evidently Divine State directly and by My Responsive Blessing of them. My devotees must (intrinsically) be profoundly conformed to Me, through their right devotional recognition of Me, their right devotional response to Me, and their right practice of the Reality-Way I have Revealed and Given—because the activity that is egoity itself must be intrinsically relinquished (and, thus, out-grown by non-use).

Unless egoity is (thus) out-grown, you cannot "Locate" Me Perfectly. You cannot "Know" Me Perfectly. Therefore, the only-by-Me Revealed and Given Reality-Way of Adidam involves many preliminary practices. It involves a process in which the psycho-physical habits of egoity, or of dissociating from the Divine Self-Nature, Self-Condition, and Self-State (or the Divine Transcendental Spiritual Nature, Condition, and State), are out-grown (or vanished, undermined, and dissolved).

Ultimately, the process of Divine Self-Realization in the Reality-Way of Adidam is a Transcendental Spiritual Process, a process of direct Awakening by Means of My Avatarically Self-Transmitted Divine Transcendental Spiritual Grace. That is how the Witness-Consciousness is Established. That is how the "Perfect Practice" of the Reality-Way of Adidam is Established. The "Perfect Practice" of the Reality-Way of Adidam is not based in some presumption that you achieve some kind of one-pointed thought or feeling or tacit power based on My clear Teaching-Arguments—such that, by (or in and of) itself, My Argument "causes" you to Realize the Transcendental Self-Condition. It is not so. True Transcendental Self-Realization Is a Transcendental Spiritual Realization, not a realization by means of mind, or in mind, nor by means of any efforts of body-mind-"self". When all efforts cease, and the Inherent Attractive Power of the Self-Existing and Self-Radiant Divine Reality is able to Break Through the barriers imposed by egoity—when that Event has occurred in My Divine Avataric Company, then the "Perfect Practice" begins.

The "Perfect Practice" of the only-by-Me Revealed and Given Reality-Way of Adidam has no conditional basis whatsoever. It is not

Established by verbal arguments. No mental foundation or categories of thinking Establish and Maintain the "Perfect Practice". Likewise, no conditional apparatus (gross, subtle, or causal), no mechanism of body or mind or psyche or conditional "root"-awareness, no exercise of faculties or structures or egoity or separate "self"—none of that establishes the "Perfect Practice" of the Reality-Way of Adidam, nor is the "Perfect Practice" dependent on any such structures or activities.

The "Perfect Practice" of the only-by-Me Revealed and Given Reality-Way of Adidam has nothing to do with the structures of the body-mind-complex, or with the activities of psycho-physical effort of any kind (however subtle). There is no exercise of faculties or structures—gross, subtle, or causal—in the "Perfect Practice" of the Reality-Way of Adidam. None whatsoever—none. The "Perfect Practice" is not kept in place by any of that, not dependent on it, not achieved by it. The "Perfect Practice" has nothing to do with any of it. In the "Perfect Practice" of the only-by-Me Revealed and Given Reality-Way of Adidam, there is no dependency on any psycho-physical conditions whatsoever.

Therefore, in the "Perfect Practice" of the Reality-Way of Adidam, there are no exercises of mind (or of the subtle person), no in-depth meditation exercises of attention, and so on. None of that has anything to do with the "Perfect Practice" of the Reality-Way of Adidam. All of that is gone beyond as a <u>preliminary</u> to the "Perfect Practice" of Adidam. There are, therefore, no psycho-physical practices or techniques in the "Perfect Practice" of Adidam.

Preliminary to the "Perfect Practice" there are, in the Reality-Way of Adidam, modes of practice that are engaged in reference to the body-mind-complex, but that Awakening Which Establishes the "Perfect Practice" of the Reality-Way of Adidam is Inherently, Perfectly, and Priorly Free of all identification with the body-mind-"self". Therefore, the "Perfect Practice" Itself simply has to do with That Which Is Transcendentally Spiritually Realized. The "Perfect Practice" of the Reality-Way of Adidam is not about identification with the body-mind-"self", such that psycho-physical exercises must be engaged in order for the "Perfect Practice" to be demonstrated.

The "Perfect Practice" of the only-by-Me Revealed and Given Reality-Way of Adidam is Spiritually Established and Transcendentally Awake. The *Ribhu Gita,* as an example of the sixth stage traditions, does not directly speak in terms of Spiritual Transmission, or Spiritual Means of Awakening. There is, however, the Blessing of the devotee by the Master. That Blessing is (essentially) the Master's willingness to Teach the devotee, and to be skillfully adept at such Teaching, so as to deal with the vagaries and the quirks of the devotee.

Thus, the Blessing of most traditional Sages is given primarily through (and as) verbal instructions—although the best of the traditional Sages have, in fact, Blessed their devotees by Means of the Silent Spiritual Blessing-Power inherent in the Sage's own State of Transcendental Self-Abiding. In the *Ribhu Gita,* chapter twenty-six is presented as the instruction given to Nidagha by the Sage Ribhu. That instruction is the Blessing and the Teaching, apart from the Master's continued positive regard and helping-efforts. There is no description in the *Ribhu Gita* of Spiritual Transmission, of Awakening by strictly Spiritual Means. So, how is Ribhu's "Abide As That" admonition actually to be Realized? How is it to be fulfilled?

As soon as this "one-thought-only" practice is described, you might presume that you are Realizing this (in some fashion or other). It somehow seems obvious. However, that presumption is simply an illusion in the body-mind-complex. As soon as some other words are said or some other "experience" happens, the mind starts wandering, instead of concentrating on the communication in the text—and, then, what happened to Realization? You see? The ego is "back in business".

"Abide As That" having been communicated over and over again, something had to be said at the end of the text, in the form of passing on a practice—because it is presumed, even in this text, that someone who hears this admonition is not (sheerly on that basis) going to Realize the Truth, just as Nidagha did not Realize the Truth. Therefore, at the end of the text, Nidagha is instructed, "Do this practice, do that practice, maintain the constant practice of this 'one thought' (or this tacit feeling-presumption), and do so on the basis of a purified body-mind-complex, which you can achieve by all kinds of disciplines otherwise known."

In the story that I have Told you, Nidagha is staying in his village, still doing traditional ritual practices of deity-worship and whatnot, and Ribhu keeps going downtown to find out if Nidagha has out-grown these practices yet. In the latest visit, Ribhu finds that Nidagha is full of notions about the "royal person", and full of "God"-ideas and all the rest of conventional "religion". Nidagha is all kinds of wide-eyed with thinking about great "this, that, and the other thing"—to the extent that he does not even recognize his own Master. He is full of grandiose thinking. He is full of egoic "self", and he is a mere beginner—even though, presumably, he has, in the past, often listened to the Reality-Teachings of the Sage Ribhu.

Thus, even this traditional text assumes that no one who hears the admonition to "Abide <u>As</u> That" over and over again is (sheerly on that basis) actually going to Realize the Truth. In that case, according to this text, how <u>does</u> someone "Abide <u>As</u> That"? One is instructed to discipline the body-mind-"self" further, by means of this one-pointed tacit affirmation. One is instructed to reach toward Realization by means of this "one thought", until Realization is Established—and, then, <u>you</u> will Abide <u>As</u> That, and (indeed) <u>you</u> will <u>Be</u> That.

However, the fact of the matter is that, in Truth, you will not. Such so-called "effective practice" is a myth. The "method" of thinking, or of somehow dealing with the mind, as if that leads to transcending the mind-state through conditional efforts, is part of the mythology of the Great Tradition of humankind. Whenever (in the history of the Great Tradition) a rare individual has truly Realized the Transcendental Self-Condition, that Realization has (Itself) never been the result of any conditional effort. Rather, true Realization (Itself) is always (Itself) the spontaneous Self-Evidence of Non-conditional, Tacit Self-Apprehension of the Intrinsic Self-Condition of Reality (Itself)—and, as such, true Realization (Itself) is always the specific Evidence of the Non-conditional Grace of Reality Itself (generally, Self-Transmitted by the Non-conditional Spiritual Blessing-Regard of an Adept-Sage).

Many hear great thoughts spoken in the mode of the philosophical assertions of the Great Tradition, in the terms of the fourth, the fifth, and the sixth stages of life—yet, they Realize nothing. Nothing except the entanglements that the communications themselves represent— entanglements with the body-mind-"self", with conditional existence, with all kinds of illusions, some of which are even referred to in the speeches of Ribhu (including the illusions of conventional "God"-ideas). The entanglements with the body-mind-"self" are mentioned specifically, numerous times. You should understand that the communication of the *Ribhu Gita* is addressed to a person who, up to that moment, has been practicing traditional temple-worship, engaged in the worshipping of mere "God"-ideas—including (in the case of Nidagha) the traditional idea (or myth) of the Divine personified as Siva. All of this is said, by Ribhu, to not be the "It" of It. "Abide <u>As</u> That in Which all of that is not, Nidagha. <u>Be</u> That Which has no 'God'-ideas in It, and no ego-ideas in It, and no 'world' in It. <u>Be</u> That—instead."

This admonition addresses much (in general) of the first five stages of life, and asserts the sixth stage of life. Nevertheless, its program for the "how-to-Realize-It" is <u>another</u> form of myth. There is no "<u>method</u>" whereby to Realize Reality Itself—because, if you are doing something in order to Realize Reality Itself, you must (first of all) <u>not</u> Realize Reality Itself, and be dissociated from It to such a degree that you would conceive of the motivation to <u>seek</u> It.

The only <u>True</u> Means to Realize the Divine Self-Nature, Self-Condition, and Self-State of Reality Itself Is That Which Is (Itself) to Be Realized. That Which Is to Be Realized Is the <u>only</u> Means of Realization. That Which Is to Be Realized must Self-Manifest, Transmit Itself, and Awaken the devotee directly to Itself. This is the only "method". There is no other true "method". All other "methods" are myths, programs, ideas—to which egos cling in order to work on attaining Realization (to one degree or another), or (otherwise) in order to gradually (or in one or another mode) purify the body-mind-complex of its encumbrances, and (thereby) reduce the burden of egoity, at least to some significant degree.

Most Perfect Realization of Reality Itself is Awakened directly by the Perfect Self-Manifestation of Reality Itself. Reality Awakens everyone to Itself, and Reality Itself Is the only Means. Most Perfect Realization of Reality Itself Is, Thus, a Divine and Avataric matter. It is a matter of Divine Avataric Transcendental Spiritual Grace and response to Divine Avataric Transcendental Spiritual Grace. It is a matter of right practice, yes—but the Ultimate matter of Most Perfect Realization has no conditional "cause" and is not a matter of "method" or of seeking.

In the only-by-Me Revealed and Given Reality-Way of Adidam, everything preliminary to the "Perfect Practice" is required as a foundation for the "Perfect Practice"—because the preliminary process is a process of out-growing egoity (which is, ultimately, simply a fabrication of mind). Nevertheless, egoity is a total psycho-physical activity, and not merely an idea in the mind. Egoity is enacted by the body, and it is represented by the body.

In My Telling of the traditional story of the encounter between the Sage Ribhu and His devotee Nidagha, I Describe the moment of apparent Awakening, wherein and whereby Nidagha becomes available to Ribhu's further instruction. The Awakening takes place in the paradoxical (and somewhat comical) confrontation between Ribhu and Nidagha then and there—in the town where Nidagha is residing, and in the circumstance of viewing the "royal person" (whoever was in power then and there), as the royal person passes by. Ribhu instructs Nidagha then and there—and Nidagha is drawn out of his "self"-deluded state when he suddenly comes to terms with the paradox of Ribhu's absurd question: "Who is this 'you' and who is this 'I' that you are referring to?"

Nidagha did not simply say, "Well, I am the guy sitting up here, and you are the guy standing down there." He could not any further "dualize" the bits of language which were being analyzed by Ribhu on this occasion, and which are summarized by this fundamental question: "Who is this 'I', and who is this 'you'?"

The point that is apparently made to Nidagha is that, in the daily interactions wherein words are exchanged, human beings make constant use of the reference to "oneself" as "I", and to "others" as "you". You do this routinely, as if you actually know what you mean by it, as if there actually is a specific (quantifiable) "I" or "you". You act as if you have actually observed—as if you thoroughly know what you mean by—"I" and "you", whereas (in fact) these are simply conventions of the language itself, that are routinely and programmatically used in exchanges between bodily evident whomevers.

The distinction between the apparent bodies is made by the language—and, therefore, by the mind. There is no actual "experiencing" of a defined "self" as "I" or a defined "self" as an "other". You never actually "experience" the Reality-"I" or the Reality-"you". These references are presumed (or used programmatically and automatically) in the language—simply meaning "this body" and "you-body".

Yet, who is being pointed at, in either case? You immediately and automatically say "you"—but you do not have to know anybody at all in order to refer to him or her as "you". If somebody just comes up to you on the street and asks you the time of day, you would immediately use the word "you" in referring to the person—just as you would use the word "I" in referring to yourself, simply as a matter of convention. Yet, you have no familiarity with the person at all.

The "you"-reference is a programmed automaticity of the language. It is not based on your having encountered someone and gotten to know him or her absolutely—such that, when you say "you", you know exactly and entirely and Really "Who" you mean. You do not employ such an exercise—and, remarkably, you have never applied such an exercise to arrive at the "I"-reference, either.

You have become included in a program of mere mummery, or a game of play-acting, wherein the players are never actually identified.

They are only referred to <u>as</u> <u>if</u> they were identified. Only the mask, the appearing body, is pointed at. The appearing body is the conditional "I", when the pointer is pointed toward the presumed "self-body"—and the appearing body is the conditional "you" when any so-called "other" is pointed to as an apparent body, a mask, a player, a mummer, a physically apparent other that is not thoroughly analyzed. However, the merely conditional (or bodily evident) referent of either the word "I" or the word "you" does not account for either the Self-Evident Reality-"I" or the Self-Evident Reality-"you". The Self-Evident Reality-"I" <u>and</u> the Self-Evident Reality-"you" <u>Is</u> Self-Existing and Self-Radiant (and Non-conditional) Consciousness (<u>Itself</u>).

Can you absolutely differentiate anyone at all from the universe? How do you "know" that non-humans are conscious? How do you "know" any other human being is conscious? Nevertheless, <u>all</u> beings and things <u>Are</u> Non-conditional Consciousness <u>Itself</u>. There is no place, no space in time, no "anything"-position, no "anyone"-position that is not the same Divine Transcendental Spiritual Conscious Light, the same Current of Self-Evidently Divine Being.

There is no anyone or anything that is not That, and (yet) the Universal Sacrifice persists—and some kinds of life-forms are going to have to be ingested by you in order for you to live. You will not be able to entirely avoid killing and ingesting other life-forms. You are ingesting such life-forms right now, just by breathing. You, in your turn, will also be devoured. Your apparent form will be used up and reduced to its elementals. The universe is a gigantic kind of meal—which is, in many respects, horrific.

Nevertheless, the universe is mummery. You have not actually differentiated an "I" from others. "I" is a presumption in language—and a presumption in mind—that is not inspected. You do not have an underlying direct awareness of "I". You have not "known" the "I". You make superficial references to the "I" that have to do only with an artificially (and merely conditionally) <u>presumed</u> identity—a mummer, a mere characterization, one-liners and shirts. "I" is not defined.

Is a breathing, ingesting, excreting body separate from the universe? Or are all events and processes evidence that the body is not separate—and not absolutely separable—from the Very Divinity in Which it is appearing? Yes, the body-mind-complex is evidence of That Reality. There is no absolute separation—no absolute separation between any apparent human individual and the universe, or between any apparent human individual and any other human (or, otherwise, non-human) individual.

You simply do not "know" others in an absolutely differentiated sense—and, yet, you refer to others as if they were defined entities, and you refer to yourself as if you are one. Yet, you have not investigated even yourself. Are you the body? Or is there more to you than the body? Would you just say, "Body is me"? Aren't you aware? Aren't you thinking? Aren't you feeling? Isn't there something more than just this body moving around? It is self-evident that there is more to it.

What is that "more" that the "I" is? Have you examined it sufficiently, come to "know" yourself sufficiently, that when you say "I" in your next conversation you will "know" what you mean? Similarly, have you so thoroughly examined every other, such that, again, in your next verbal exchange with anyone at all, you will "know" what and who you mean when you say "you" to someone else?

No, you will not. And that is what Nidagha realized: that these categories of "I" and "you", and so forth—"up" and "down", one or another identified as this or that—are simply conventions of mind, and they are not based on prior inspection of that to which the words seem to refer. The language is talking as you. The language has its own rules, its own inevitabilities. It goes on—on its own. There is no one thinking it, but there are presumptions programmed into it that govern what is said.

When there are no egoic (or limiting) presumptions, then the language manifests spontaneously—but egolessly. In that event, language is transparent to the Divine Self-Nature, Self-Condition, and Self-State Itself. However, when the language is being manipulated by lesser presumptions, then the language is a manifestation of egoity, and of many and various kinds of limitations. Yet, it is still the language talking.

Nidagha did not "know" who "I" is or who "you" is. He had not inspected the identities or the differences in any absolute sense. He was simply babbling the conventions of speech—and he had no true idea of what he was talking about. None. Just as you do not have the slightest clue as to what you are talking about—ever. You do not "know" what a single thing is. You do not "know" who you are. You do not "know" who anyone else is. You do not "know" what anything is.

You do not "know" what Reality Is. You do not "know" what the "world" is. You do not "know" anything. You are a talking fool, you see. It is an absurdity—this mummery of language and of "experiencing" and of trouble. It is foolishness. It is non-Reality. It is mummery only. That mummery takes the form of the first six stages of life.

All the modes of manifestation and conversation that correspond to the sixth stage of life are modes of egoity. Therefore, even the conversations between Sages and their devotees are mummery. All is mummery, except for the sheer Self-Evidence of Reality Itself, directly Self-Manifested, without any introduction of limitation.

The Mode of My Person and My Transcendental Spiritual Self-Transmission is wordless, actionless, direct. Fundamentally, then, one could say that It Is Silent, or that It goes on in spite of anything else that may appear to be going on—because It has (Itself) nothing to do with any of that appearance. Therefore, whatever may be appearing makes no "difference" whatsoever. I Am nevertheless (or Always Already) Present and Self-Manifested, Self-Radiant, Self-Transmitted to those who devotionally recognize Me and devotionally respond to Me—and no special conditions are required for Me to Do any of That, Which is, in the merely conditional sense, no doing at all.

Therefore, none of the errors of the first six stages of life pertain to the "Perfect Practice" of the only-by-Me Revealed and Given Reality-Way of Adidam, or to the truly "Radical" (or Always "At-the-Root") Reality-Way of Its Realization. The even more that must be Said about the "Perfect Practice" of the Reality-Way of Adidam has to do with Its Most Ultimate (or seventh stage) manifestation, or the third stage of the "Perfect Practice".

What I have Said so far is a sufficient Address to the contrast between the "Perfect Practice" of the Reality-Way of Adidam and the Non-dualist tradition of the Sages. That Non-dualist tradition functions entirely within the framework of the six developmental stages of life. The sixth stage of life is the Ultimate development of the traditional Great Process. At last, the sixth stage of life gestures Beyond the body-mind-"self", and Beyond the causal "root" (or causal body)—or would be stepped Beyond the causal "root"—but it attempts to do so by an act of dissociation, or an act of Transcendental Self-Identification that goes no further.

The "Perfect Practice", or the Perfect Demonstration of the only-by-Me Revealed and Given Reality-Way of Adidam, exceeds even the first six stages of life altogether—the entire context of egoity, of body-mind-"self", of conditionality.

Divine Self-Abiding, Priorly Self-Established, is the context of the only-by-Me Revealed and Given seventh stage of life of the Reality-Way of Adidam.

There are no conditional dependencies, no "practices", in the only-by-Me Revealed and Given seventh stage of life.

In the only-by-Me Revealed and Given seventh stage of life, there is simply the spontaneous Self-Evidence, or spontaneous Reality-Event, of Self-Abiding Divine Self-Recognition of all that is apparently "known", of all that apparently arises as "experience".

Self-Abiding Divine Self-Recognition Transcends the apparent conditional evidence of moment to moment—all the evidence that takes the form of separateness, relatedness, "otherness", and "difference".

All conditional "experiencing" or "knowing" has these four characteristics—coincidentally.

Wherever there is the "one", there is the "other".

Separateness, relatedness, "otherness", and "difference" are the characteristics of egoity, of "self"-contraction, of bondage, of non-Reality.

These four characteristics are inherently transcended in the only-by-Me Revealed and Given seventh stage of life (or the third stage of the "Perfect Practice" of the Reality-Way of Adidam).

All that appears to be "known" has these four characteristics—and (in the context of the only-by-Me Revealed and Given seventh stage of life) is Divinely Self-Recognized Inherently, coincident with its apparent arising.

When "it" is Divinely Self-Recognized, all conditional arising is merely apparent, non-necessary, non-binding, and (effectively) non-existent.

No "world", no "other", no Divine "Other", no conditional existence whatsoever.

Only the One Indivisible Divine Conscious Light.

Everything apparently arising is Divinely Self-Recognized as a merely apparent modification of That.

Abiding <u>As</u> That is the Self-Evidence that is the basis of the only-by-Me Revealed and Given seventh stage of life.

Self-Abiding Divine Self-Recognition of all that arises is the Demonstration of the seventh stage of life.

Self-Abiding Divine Self-Recognition is the Unique and Ultimate Demonstration of the only-by-Me Revealed and Given Reality-Way of Adidam.

That Demonstration Exceeds all of the Great Tradition.

That Demonstration is not ever found in the Great Tradition.

The only-by-Me Revealed and Given seventh stage of life spontaneously shows itself through the Demonstration of Divine Transfiguration, Divine Transformation, Divine Indifference, and (Most Ultimately) Divine Translation.[1] These are the characteristics of Realization unique to the only-by-Me Revealed and Given Reality-Way of Adidam, the Avatarically Given Reality-Way of Adidam, the Divinely Given Perfect Reality-Way of Adidam.

These aspects of Realization are not referred to in the *Ribhu Gita*, or in the sixth stage tradition (altogether), or in any of the traditions of the first six stages of life—Non-dualist or otherwise. The only-by-Me Revealed and Given seventh stage Demonstration is the Unique Divine Demonstration that is the All-Completing Dimension of the Reality-Way of Adidam.

I have just Summarized the only-by-Me Revealed and Given seventh stage of life—which is the Ultimate Unique Characteristic of the "Perfect Practice" of the Reality-Way of Adidam, in contrast to the Non-dualist sixth stage tradition of the Sages. My Summary is, in particular, a Criticism of the limitations inherent in the sixth stage "point of view", as communicated by the *Ribhu Gita* and by all other traditional sixth stage texts—whether Advaitic, or Buddhist, or coming from any other sixth stage tradition.

There are limitations in all the traditions, and those limitations are the limitations of egoity. They are the limitations of the developmental stages of life. Each tradition speaks on the basis of the patterns of egoity and the stages of life that spring from the psycho-physical structures with which the human entity is egoically "self"-identified. Each tradition speaks on the fundamental basis of one or the other of the first six stages of life that could be called its "leading edge"—the fundamental stance or dimension of what the tradition declares to be Reality and Realization.

The only-by-Me Revealed and Given Reality-Way of Adidam exceeds all traditions, all developmental stages of life, all of egoity. This is the nature of its Perfection. It is not a human or "worldly" perfection. It is the Inherent Perfection that is the characteristic of Reality Itself. Reality Is Divine. Reality Is Truth. There is no other Divine Truth, and no other Truth at all.

The Divine Is the Self-Evident, Non-"Different" Reality in and of and <u>As</u> Which everything and everyone is seeming to appear. This must be Realized—and can be Realized—by Direct Divine Transcendental Spiritual Grace, Avatarically Given in the midst of the right life of right practice of the only-by-Me Revealed and Given Reality-Way of Adidam.

XIII

ADVAITA BUDDHA DHARMA[1] OF
AVATAR ADI DA SAMRAJ

The Only-By-Me Revealed and Given Advaitayana Buddhist (or Buddhayana Advaitist) Summation of the Self-Evident Reality-Truth of Non-"Difference" Itself and the Self-Evident Reality-Truth of the Non-"Difference" Between "Advaitic Truth" and "Buddhist Truth":

The Intrinsically Self-Evident Reality-Condition of any and all conditions and the Intrinsically Self-Evident Reality-Condition <u>Prior</u> to any and all conditions <u>Is</u> One and <u>Is</u> the Same.

APPENDIX

Avatar Adi Da's Revelation of the Seven Stages of Life

Avatar Adi Da Samraj has "mapped" the potential developmental course of human experience as it unfolds through the gross, subtle, and causal dimensions of the being, describing this course in terms of six stages of life. These six stages of life, he explains, account for, and correspond with, all possible orientations to religion and culture that have arisen in human history. His own Divine Avataric Revelation—the Realization of the "Bright", or Reality Itself, Prior to all experience—he describes as the seventh stage of life.

The first three (or foundation) stages of life constitute the ordinary course of human adaptation—bodily, emotional, and mental growth. Each of the first three stages of life takes approximately seven years to be established. Every individual who lives to an adult age inevitably adapts (although, generally speaking, only partially) to the first three stages of life. In the general case, this is where the developmental process stops—at the gross level of adaptation. Traditions based fundamentally on beliefs and moral codes (without direct experience of the dimensions beyond the material world) belong to this foundation level of human development.

The fourth stage of life is characterized, in its beginnings, by a deep impulse to communion with the Divine, felt to be a great "Other" in whom the being aspires to become absorbed through devotional love and service. In the fifth stage of life, attention naturally moves into the domain of subtle experience and seeks the Samadhi states associated with ascending energy in the spinal line. The esoteric Spiritual traditions associated with mystical experience correspond with this higher level of human potential.

The Realizer of the sixth stage of life is focused in the causal depth of the being. He or she identifies with Consciousness (in profound states of meditation) by excluding all awareness of phenomena, both gross and subtle. And, when phenomena do arise, the sixth stage Realizer stands as the "Witness" of phenomena, unimplicated by body, mind, or world. Such is genuine Realization of the sixth stage of life. However, Avatar Adi Da has also pointed out the tendency in some traditional circles to attempt to identify with Consciousness (or "the Self") based on a "talking"-school approach that is founded in mind, rather than genuine Realization.

The seventh stage of life, or the Realization of the "Bright" Reality Revealed through the Incarnation of Avatar Adi Da Samraj, transcends this entire course of human potential. In that Awakening, it is suddenly, tacitly Realized that there is no "difference" between Consciousness Itself and the objects of Consciousness. Thus, the seventh stage Realization wipes away every trace of dissociation from the body-mind and the world. Consciousness Itself, or Being Itself, Is all there is, and Consciousness Itself is found to be Radiant, or Love-Bliss-Full. Thus, every "thing" and every "one" that appears is inherently recognized to be a mere modification of the One Divine "Brightness" (or the Divine Conscious Light).

NOTES

INTRODUCTION

1. Avatar Adi Da describes the human body-mind in terms of the system of five sheaths (or koshas) first described in the *Taittiriya Upanishad:* the physical body (annamayakosha); the system of life-energy and sensory perception (pranamayakosha); the sense-based mind (manomayakosha); the root-mind (vijnanamayakosha); and the ultimate hierarchical root of the conditionally manifested "self" (anandamayakosha). See Adi Da Samraj, *Santosha Adidam* (Middletown, Calif.: The Dawn Horse Press, 2001).

2. Further explication of these and other essential terms and concepts used in this book can be found in the glossary following the text.

3. See the glossary for an explanation of the particular use of this term.

4. Translated from Swamijir Katha in Bengali, included in *Reminiscences of Swami Vivekananda* (Almora, India: Advaita Ashrama, 1961), 51.

5. *The Crest Jewel of Wisdom* (*Viveka-Chudamani*), attributed to Shri Shankacharya, translated by A. J. Alston (London: Shanti Sadan, 1997), 176.

6. Ramana Maharshi (1879–1950) is regarded by many as the greatest Indian Sage of the twentieth century.

7. Adi Da Samraj, *My "Bright" Word* (Middletown, Calif.: The Dawn Horse Press, 2005), 82.

8. Adi Da Samraj, *The Knee of Listening* (Middletown, Calif.: The Dawn Horse Press, 2004).

9. "Advaitayana Buddhism" and "Buddhayana Advaitism" are terms that indicate the unique sympathetic likeness of the Reality-Way of Adidam to the traditions of Advaitism (or Advaita Vedanta) and Buddhism. Advaitayana Buddhism

is the non-dual ("Advaita") way ("yana", literally "vehicle") of perfect awakening ("Buddhism"). Buddhayana Advaitism is the way ("yana") of non-dual Truth ("Advaitism") revealed and given by the enlightened one ("Buddha"). Adidam is neither an outgrowth of the historical tradition of Buddhism nor of the historical tradition of Advaitism. It is the unique revelation of Avatar Adi Da Samraj, which fulfills both the traditional Buddhist aspiration for absolute freedom from the bondage of the egoic self and the traditional Advaitic aspiration for absolute identity with the Divine Self.

Chapter I. To Realize Nirvana Is To Realize The True Self

1. Such as the *Udana* and the *Digha Nikaya*.
2. Quoted by K. N. Jayatilleke, in *The Message of the Buddha* (New York: The Free Press, 1975), 125, 126, and 123, respectively.

Chapter V. What Is Required To Realize The Non-Dual Truth?

1. Avatar Adi Da has referred to Atmananda (Krishna Menon) and Nisargadata Maharaj as examples of such teachers.
2. The earliest Upanishads are believed to have been composed in the eighth to seventh centuries BCE. The early Upanishadic era was a remarkable period of wisdom-instruction about Transcendental Realization from the Sages and traditions that gave rise to the Upanishadic texts.
3. Avatar Adi Da Samraj points out that the traditional tantric paths are significantly different than conventional and Westernized presumptions about tantra. Here, Adi Da is referring to esoteric tantra in its authentic (and, in some cases, yogically sexually active) traditional forms. Some (though not all) schools of traditional tantra were non-celibate. In those schools, sexuality was engaged in as a highly disciplined yogic exercise—outside the context of the pair-bondage and the familial responsibilities that are traditionally associated with sexual activity.
4. Swami Gnanananda Giri (?–1974) was a wandering sannyasin and Advaitin who eventually established an ashram in south India. Swami Gnanananda taught both Advaitic self-enquiry and preparatory practices of service and devotion. His full biography is published as *Sadguru Gnanananda: His Life, Personality, and Teachings,* by his devotees (Bombay: Bharatiya Vidya Bhavan, 1979).
5. "Jnana" means "knowledge". Jnana Samadhi is the meditative state characteris-

tic of the sixth stage of life. Produced by the intentional withdrawal of attention from the conditional body-mind-self and its relations, Jnana Samadhi is the conditional, temporary realization of the transcendental Self-Condition (or Consciousness Itself), exclusive of any perception (or cognition) of world, objects, relations, body, mind, or separate-self-sense.

6. The Sanskrit word "Samadhi" traditionally denotes various exalted states that appear in the context of esoteric meditation and realization. The Sanskrit term "Nirvikalpa Samadhi" literally means "meditative ecstasy without form", or "deep meditative concentration (or absorption) in which there is no perception of form (or defined experiential content)". "Sahaja" is Sanskrit for "born together, innate, or natural". Thus, "Sahaja Nirvikalpa Samadhi" means "innate samadhi without form". Avatar Adi Da notes that the fourth, fifth, sixth, and seventh stages of life each have a characteristic mode of "Sahaja Nirvikalpa Samadhi". For more about the sixth stage mode of samadhi, see note 5 above.

7. "Open Eyes" is Avatar Adi Da's technical synonym for the realization of seventh stage Sahaja Nirvikalpa Samadhi, or Divine Enlightenment. The phrase graphically describes the non-exclusive, non-inward, prior state of Realization, in which the Realizer is identified non-conditionally with the Divine Self-Reality, while also allowing whatever arises to appear in that Divine Consciousness. This term is placed in quotation marks to indicate that Avatar Adi Da uses it with the specific technical meaning described here (rather than any of the more commonly accepted general meanings).

See also note 6 above for a definition of "Sahaja Nirvikalpa Samadhi".

8. This "point of view" is comprehensively expressed in the writings of Swami Satchidanandendra Saraswati, in such texts as *The Basic Tenets of Sankara Vedanta* (Holenarsipur, India: Adhyatma Prakasha Karyalaya, 1996).

9. See text by Swami Satchidanandendra listed in note 8 above.

10. Many traditional Advaitic texts are attributed to Shankara, but much scholarly controversy surrounds the issue of which texts were actually written by him. There is a general consensus that Shankara was the author of the commentaries on the *Brahmasutras,* the *Upanishads,* and the *Bhagavad Gita* that are attributed to him, as well as the independent work *Upadesasahasri.* Among the representative translations of these works are:

Brahma Sutras (With Text, Word-for-Word Translation, English Rendering, Comments According to the Commentary of Sri Sankara, and Index), by Swami Vireswarananda (Kolkata: Advaita Ashram, 2001).

The Upanishads, by Swami Nikhilananda, with notes and explanations based on the commentary of Sri Sankaracharya (New York: Ramakrishna-Vivekananda Center); Vol. 1: *Katha, Isa, Kena, and Mundaka,* 5th ed., 1990; Vol. 2: *Svetasvatara, Prasna, and Mandukya with Gaudapada's Karika,* 3rd ed., 1990; Vol. 3: *Aitareya and Brihadaranyaka,* 3rd ed., 1990; Vol. 4: *Taittiriya and Chhandogya,* 2nd ed., 1979.

Sri Sankara's Gita Bhashya (*Sri Sankaracharya's Commentary on the* Gita), translation by C. V. Ramachandra Aiyar (Bombay: Bharatiya Vidya Bhavan, 1988).

Upadesa Sahasri: A Thousand Teachings, in Two Parts (Prose and Poetry), of Sri Sankaracarya, translated into English, with explanatory notes, by Swami Jagadananda (Madras [Chennai]: Sri Ramakrishna Math, 2003).

CHAPTER VIII. MY RENDERINGS OF THE ANCIENT REALITY-TEACHINGS

1. These are Avatar Adi Da's principal communications of "Perfect Practice" Reality-Teaching. *Eleutherios* is the principal text in the book of the same name—*Eleutherios (The Only Truth That Sets The Heart Free)* (Middletown, Calif.: The Dawn Horse Press, 2006). *The Lion Sutra* is published as sutra 56 of *The Dawn Horse Testament* (Middletown, Calif.: The Dawn Horse Press, 2004).

2. The *Brahma Sutras* is a text in which the teachings of Vedanta are presented in a logical order, with the intention of clarifying and systematizing the Upanishadic teachings.

3. This is an allusion to Avatar Adi Da's literary work *The Mummery Book* (Book One of *The Orpheum*). The "neighborhood-wars" stem from the presumption of absolute separation, such that every individual "declares" himself or herself a "separate state", and "wages war" even on his or her own neighbors.

4. The Jains believe that the universe is eternal—never "born" and never ceasing. In the endless cycle of ever-changing ages that is the manifest universe, Jains describe the appearance of Tirthankars, or heroes, who appear to restore the religion of Jainism when it is lost. Mahavir (599–527 BCE; great [maha] hero [vir]) is said to have been the twenty-fourth Tirthankar of the present age (or time-cycle).

5. For example, Theravadin Buddhists celebrate twenty-eight buddhas, culminating in the appearance of Gotama. Buddhist lore also includes many "Jataka tales", which celebrate the reputed past lives of the "historical Buddha", Gotama.

6. Mahavaykas meaning "Thou Art That" and "I Am Brahman", respectively. These are two of the four classic Upanishadic mahavakyas.

7. Originally published in Avatar Adi Da's text *The Enlightenment of the Whole Body* (Middletown, Calif.: The Dawn Horse Press, 1978), in an essay entitled "The Living God and the 'Void' of Self-Realization".

8. The complete essay from which Avatar Adi Da is quoting appears as chapter VII: "The Five Declarations of Ultimate Knowledge".

9. Avatar Adi Da characteristically makes this sound to convey blessing.

10. *Eleutherios* appears in the full text of *The Gnosticon,* from which the materials in this book have been drawn (*The Gnosticon* is forthcoming from the Dawn Horse Press). *Eleutherios* has also been published as the principal text in the book of the same name—*Eleutherios (The Only Truth That Sets The Heart Free)* (Middletown, Calif.: The Dawn Horse Press, 2006).

CHAPTER X. REALITY (ITSELF) IS ALL THE GOD THERE IS

1. While the exact dates for the purported lifetime of Gotama Saykamuni are not clear, most modern scholars believe he lived between 563 BCE and 483 BCE.

2. For Avatar Adi Da's presentation of "Perfect Practice" Reality-Teachings, see *Eleutherios (The Only Truth That Sets The Heart Free)* (Middletown, Calif.: The Dawn Horse Press, 2006).

CHAPTER XII. SIXTH-STAGE METHOD VERSUS PERFECT PRACTICE

1. Avatar Adi Da has revealed that, in the seventh stage of life, the process of Divine Enlightenment is demonstrated through four stages: Divine Transfiguration, Divine Transformation, Divine Indifference, and Divine Translation. See Adi Da Samraj, *The Seven Stages Of Life* (Middletown, Calif.: The Dawn Horse Press, 2000).

CHAPTER XIII. ADVAITA BUDDHA DHARMA OF AVATAR ADI DA SAMRAJ

1. The non-dual (Advaita) teaching (Dharma) of the enlightened one (Buddha).

GLOSSARY

anatta—A Pali word equivalent to Sanskrit "anatman", meaning "no self". Anatta is the Buddhist teaching that no specifiable, unchanging self (or soul-characteristic) is discoverable in the context of conditional existence.

atman / Atman—Sanskrit for "self", indicating the "individual self" when lowercase and the Divine "Self" when uppercase.

Brahman—In the Hindu tradition, Brahman is the ultimate Divine Reality that is the source and substance of all things, all worlds, and all beings.

Brahmanic Atman—The supreme "Self" of all beings, things, and worlds.

"Bright"—By the word "Bright" (and its variations, such as "Brightness"), Avatar Adi Da refers to the Divine Reality that was demonstrated from his birth. In infancy, as soon as he acquired the capability of language, Avatar Adi Da gave the name "the 'Bright'" to his own state. This term is placed in quotation marks to indicate that Avatar Adi Da uses it with the specific meaning described here.

causal (dimension)—*See* **gross, subtle, causal (dimensions)**.

"create" / "Creator"—Avatar Adi Da Samraj places the word "create" (and its variants) in quotation marks when he wishes to indicate the sense of "so to speak"—communicating that, in reality, any particular "thing" is not truly (but only apparently) appearing "out of nothing" or being caused to appear (or "created").

Darshan—"Darshan" (the Hindi derivative of Sanskrit "darshana") literally means "seeing", "sight of", or "vision of". "Darshan" is used to describe devotional sighting of the Realizer by the devotee.

dharma—Sanskrit for "duty", "virtue", "law". The word "dharma" is commonly

192

used to refer to the many esoteric paths by which human beings seek the Truth. In its fullest sense, and when capitalized, "Dharma" means the complete fulfillment of duty—the living of the Divine Law. By extension, "Dharma" means a spiritual teaching, including its disciplines and practices.

"difference"—The root of the egoic presumption of separateness—in contrast with the Realization of Oneness, or non-"difference". This term is placed in quotation marks to indicate that Avatar Adi Da uses it in the "so to speak" sense. He is communicating (by means of the quotation marks) that, in reality, there is no such thing as "difference", even though it appears to be the case from the point of view of ordinary human perception.

Divine Self-Recognition—Divine Self-Recognition is the ego-transcending and world-transcending "Intelligence" of Reality in relation to all conditional phenomena. In the seventh stage of life, one simply abides as the Divine Conscious Light, and freely "Self-Recognizes" (or inherently and instantly and most perfectly comprehends and perceives) all phenomena (including body, mind, conditional self, and conditional world) as transparent (or merely apparent), and unnecessary, and inherently non-binding modifications of the same Conscious Light.

ego-"I"—The presumption of separate and separative existence. The "I" is placed in quotation marks to indicate that it is used by Avatar Adi Da in the "so to speak" sense. He is communicating (by means of the quotation marks) that, in reality, there is no such thing as the separate "I", even though it appears to be the case from the point of view of ordinary human perception.

feeling of relatedness—The presumption of separation that is at the root of egoic existence.

Great Tradition—Avatar Adi Da's term for the total inheritance of human, cultural, religious, magical, mystical, spiritual, and transcendental paths, philosophies, and testimonies, from all the eras and cultures of humanity—which inheritance has (in the present era of worldwide communication) become the common legacy of humankind.

gross, subtle, causal (dimensions)—Avatar Adi Da (in agreement with certain esoteric schools) describes conditional existence as having three fundamental dimensions—gross, subtle, and causal.

"Gross" means "made up of material (or physical) elements". The gross (or physical) dimension is, therefore, associated with the physical body. The gross dimension is also associated with experience in the waking state and, as Avatar Adi Da reveals, with the frontal line of the body-mind and with the left side of the heart (or the gross physical heart).

The subtle dimension, which is senior to and pervades the gross dimension, consists of the etheric (or personal life-energy) functions, the lower mental functions (including the conscious mind, the subconscious mind, and the unconscious mind) and higher mental functions (of discriminative mind, mentally presumed egoity, and will), and is associated with experience in the dreaming state. In the human psycho-physical structure, the subtle dimension is primarily associated with the middle station of the heart (or the heart chakra), the spinal line, the brain core, and the subtle centers of mind in the higher brain.

The causal dimension is senior to both the gross and the subtle dimensions. It is the root of attention, or the root-sense of existence as a separate self. The causal dimension is associated with the right side of the heart, specifically with the sinoatrial node, or "pacemaker" (the psycho-physical source of the heartbeat). Its corresponding state of consciousness is the formless awareness of deep sleep.

"late-time" (or "dark" epoch)—Avatar Adi Da uses the terms "late-time" and "'dark' epoch" to describe the present era—in which doubt of the Divine (and of anything at all beyond mortal existence) is more and more pervading the entire world, and the self-interest of the separate individual is more and more regarded to be the ultimate principle of life.

Mahavakya—There are four principal "great (maha) statements (vakyas)" in the Upanishadic tradition of India. All are intended to be expressions of the realization of Oneness with the Supreme Divine Self. Each mahavakya is connected with one of the four Vedas. Thus, "prajnanam brahma" ("Consciousness is Brahman") occurs in the *Aitareya Upanishad* of the *Rig Veda;* "ayam atma brahma" ("This self is Brahman") occurs in the *Mandukya Upanishad* of the *Atharva Veda;* "tat tvam asi" ("That thou art") occurs in the *Chandogya Upanishad* of the *Sama Veda;* and "aham brahmasmi" ("I am Brahman") occurs in the *Brihadaranyaka Upanishad* of the *Yajur Veda.*

Mahavir—(599–527 BCE) A contemporary of Gotama Sakyamuni, Mahavir is regarded as the founder of Jainism.

manana—The second of the stages of traditional Advaitic practice, indicating examination of the Advaitic teaching arguments to the point of intuitive understanding. *See also* **sravana** and **nididhyasana.**

Most Perfect / Most Ultimate—Avatar Adi Da uses the phrase "Most Perfect(ly)" in the sense of "Absolutely Perfect(ly)". Similarly, the phrase "Most Ultimate(ly)" is equivalent to "Absolutely Ultimate(ly)". "Most Perfect(ly)" and "Most Ultimate(ly)" are always references to the seventh (or Divinely Enlightened) stage of life. Adi Da uses "Perfect(ly)" and "Ultimate(ly)" (without "Most") to refer to the practice and realization in the context of the "Perfect Practice" of the Reality-Way of Adidam (or, when making reference to other traditions, to practice and realization in the context of the sixth stage of life).

Nagarjuna—One of the most influential figures in the history of Buddhism, Nagarjuna (ca. 150–250 CE) was an Indian philosopher and the founder of the Madhyamaka school of Mahayana Buddhism.

nididhyasana—The third (and final) of the stages of traditional Advaitic practice, indicating deep contemplation of Truth to the point of Realization. *See also* **sravana** and **manana**.

Nirvana—A Buddhist term for the Unqualified Reality beyond suffering, ego, birth, and death.

"Perfect Practice"—The "Perfect Practice" is Avatar Adi Da's technical term for the discipline of the most mature stages of practice in the Reality-Way of Adidam. The "Perfect Practice" is practice in the domain of Consciousness Itself (as opposed to practice from the point of view of the body or the mind). The "Perfect Practice" unfolds in three phases, the third of which is Divine Enlightenment. This term is placed in quotation marks to indicate that Avatar Adi Da uses it with the specific technical meaning described here.

"radical"—Derived from the Latin "radix" (meaning "root"), "radical" principally means "irreducible", "fundamental", or "relating to the origin". Thus, Avatar Adi Da defines "radical" as "at-the-root". Because Adi Da Samraj uses "radical" in this literal sense, it appears in quotation marks in his writings, in order to distinguish his usage from the common reference to an extreme (often political) view.

Ramana Maharshi—Ramana Maharshi (1879–1950) is regarded by many as the greatest Indian sage of the twentieth century. Following a spontaneous death-like event in his teens, he abandoned home for a life of spiritual practice. Eventually, an ashram was established around him at Tiruvannamalai in South India.

Ribhu—An ancient sage of India, who appears in the Puranic and Upanishadic literature. Although reputed to have been an actual individual, there is no concrete historical information on Ribhu, and the stories about him tend toward myth (for example, in the *Visnu Purana*, Ribhu is said to be the "mind son" of the Hindu God Brahma).

Samadhi—The Sanskrit word "Samadhi" traditionally denotes various exalted states that appear in the context of esoteric meditation and realization. Avatar Adi Da teaches that, for his devotees, samadhi is, even more simply and fundamentally, the enjoyment of his Divine State (or "Divine Samadhi"), which is experienced (even from the beginning of the practice of Adidam) through ego-transcending devotional communion with Adi Da.

samsara—The Buddhist and Hindu term for the conditional realm of birth and change and death.

sannyasa / sannyasin—"Sannyasin" is a Sanskrit term for an ascetic renunciate, one who has relinquished all bonds and social obligation. In the Reality-Way of Adidam, renunciation (or sannyasa) does not involve asceticism.

Self-Existing and Self-Radiant—"Self-Existing" and "Self-Radiant" are terms describing the two fundamental aspects of the One Divine Person (or Reality)—Existence (or Being, or Consciousness) Itself, and Radiance (or Energy, or Light) Itself.

Self-Recognition. *See* **Divine Self-Recognition.**

Shakti—A Sanskrit term for the spiritual Energy or Power of the Divine.

Shankara—(ca. 788–820) A revered Hindu Sage who is regarded as the founder of the school of Advaita Vedanta.

sravana—The first of the stages of traditional Advaitic practice, indicating attentive "listening" to (or intensive study of) the Advaitic teachings. *See also* **manana** and **nididhyasana.**

stages of life—Avatar Adi Da Samraj describes the experiences and realizations of humankind in terms of seven stages of life. *See* the appendix.

subtle (dimension)—*See* **gross, subtle, causal (dimensions).**

"talking" school (vs. "practicing" school)—"'Talking' school" is a phrase used by Avatar Adi Da to refer to those in any tradition of sacred life whose approach is characterized by talking, thinking, reading, and philosophical analysis and debate, or even meditative enquiry or reflection, without a concomitant and foundation discipline of body, emotion, mind, and breath.

He contrasts the "talking" school with the "practicing" school approach—
"practicing" schools involving those who are committed to the ordeal of real
ego-transcending discipline, under the guidance of a true guru.

Tcha—A sound that Avatar Adi Da characteristically makes to convey blessing.

Witness / Witness-Consciousness—When Consciousness is free of identification with the body-mind, it stands in its natural "Position" as the conscious "Witness" of all that arises to and in and as the body-mind.

In the Reality-Way of Adidam, the stable realization of the "Witness-
Position" is a gift from Avatar Adi Da, made possible by (and necessarily following upon) the reception of Adi Da's Transcendental Spiritual
Blessing. The stable Realization of the Witness-Position is the characteristic of the first stage of the "Perfect Practice". Further elaboration can be
found in *The Dawn Horse Testament* (Middletown, Calif.: The Dawn Horse
Press, 2004).

About Avatar Adi Da Samraj

From his birth (on Long Island, New York, in 1939), Avatar Adi Da Samraj manifested unique signs of spiritual illumination. "Avatar" means "one who has crossed down from the divine realm, entering the world in order to bless and liberate beings". Throughout his first two years, Adi Da Samraj existed in a state of constant spiritual radiance and joy, without any sense of separate self (or ego). However, it became obvious to him that others did not enjoy that state. So, in a specific moment at two years of age, he spontaneously chose to "become" a human ego, to become the human child that his parents had named "Franklin Jones". He did this in order to experience, firsthand, what the human "problem" is, and to discover how that "problem" can be overcome. His impulse was to make it possible for everyone to enjoy the supremely blissful state of divine "Brightness" that he had known since birth.

Avatar Adi Da's remarkable gesture at two years old initiated His effort to "learn" and understand human existence. That effort was to last twenty-eight years.

Adi Da Samraj graduated from Columbia University in 1961, with a BA in philosophy (including much concentration in both art and literature), and from Stanford University in 1966, with an MA in English literature. His master's thesis, a study of core issues in modernism, focused on the literary experiments of Gertrude Stein and on the modernist painters of the same period.

In 1964, Adi Da Samraj began a period of intensive practice under a succession of spiritual masters in the United States and India—Rudi (or Swami Rudrananda), Swami Muktananda, and (on the subtle planes) Bhagavan Nityananda (who had left the body in 1960). In relationship with his human teachers, Adi Da Samraj experienced every form of mystical or transcendental attainment that has ever been sought by human beings, in East or West. When that great tour of the human spiritual quest was complete, he knew that none of the traditional "answers" were "it"—because none of them were equivalent to the egoless state of perfect divine "Brightness" he had known at birth.

Finally, on September 10, 1970, Adi Da Samraj spontaneously became reestablished in the continuous state of illumination that was his condition at birth. He perfectly "regained" what he had (at two years of age) volunteered to "lose". Now he was equipped with the fullest possible experiential knowledge of the human condition and the process of spiritual growth, so he could begin his work of teaching others.

Adi Da Samraj formally began to teach in 1972, creating a vast repository of wisdom in living dialogue with those who approached him as devotees. To date, his literary, philosophical, and practical writings consist of over sixty published books—many internationally acclaimed. In the early 1970s, Alan Watts, writer of numerous books on religion and philosophy, acknowledged Adi Da Samraj as "a rare being", adding "It is obvious, from all sorts of subtle details, that he knows what IT's all about." In more recent years, religious studies scholar Jeffrey Kripal commented, "The writings of Adi Da Samraj are the most doctrinally thorough, the most philosophically sophisticated, the most culturally challenging, and the most creatively original literature on radical non-duality currently available in the English language."

Avatar Adi Da's formal teaching-work also lasted for twenty-eight years—from 1972 to 2000. During this time, he did absolutely everything necessary to create an entirely new spiritual way of life—the way of devotional and spiritual relationship to him, to which he gave the name "the Reality-Way of Adidam". He called into being a new form of human culture—with its unique forms of worship, artistic creativity, and cooperative living, all based in the life of devotional communion with him.

While the end of Avatar Adi Da's early-life period was signaled by the event of his re-awakening, the end of his period of teaching was signaled by a sequence of events that occurred over a span of years, ending in the year 2000. Each of these events was a profound spiritual crisis, associated (in each case) with the near-death of his body. After each of these events, his being was dramatically restructured, and the nature of his work in the world was transformed. In recent years, Adi Da has fully relinquished his work of teaching. His "participation" in the world has become simply the pure spiritual radiating of the "Bright" state that was his illumined experience at birth and always.

Beginning particularly in the year 2000, Avatar Adi Da turned, with great intensity, to the creation of artistic works. As he explains, his art is intended to communicate exactly the same truth as his verbal teachings—but through the more intuitive mode of visual perception. In 2007, his exhibition "Transcendental Realism: The Art of Adi Da Samraj" was acclaimed at the Venice Biennale, and in 2008 his exhibition was the centerpiece of the "Winter in Florence" art festival.

Adi Da Samraj lives independently in his island-hermitage in Fiji, where he constantly works to spiritually bless those who approach him and to express the truth of existence through modes of communication to which all human beings can respond.

NOTE: For a full account of the life of Adi Da Samraj, see his spiritual autobiography, *The Knee of Listening* (Middletown, Calif.: The Dawn Horse Press, 2004), or *The Avatar of What Is* by Carolyn Lee (Middletown, Calif.: The Dawn Horse Press, 2007).

THE REALITY-WAY OF ADIDAM

In his many books, Avatar Adi Da offers his revelation of "Reality-Truth", a revelation that covers the human, spiritual, transcendental, and divine dimensions of existence. Adi Da Samraj invites everyone to read and consider his teachings, and to enjoy the benefits of such study. However, his principal offering is the Reality-Way of Adidam, the way of life for those who choose to take a formal vow of devotion and become his devotee. Avatar Adi Da Samraj has said, since the beginning of his public work of teaching devotees (in 1972), "I offer you a relationship, not a technique." The relationship to Adi Da Samraj—recognized by the devotee as the revealer of Reality-Truth and the giver of Liberation—is the basis and the means of the practice of Adidam.

> *Adidam is not a conventional "religion".*
> *Adidam is not a conventional way of life.*
> *Adidam is about the transcending of the ego-"I".*
> *Adidam is about the Freedom of Divine Self-*
>   *Realization.*
>
> *Adidam is not based on mythology or belief.*
> *Adidam is a Reality-practice.*
> *Adidam is a "reality consideration", in which all the*
>   *modes of egoity are intrinsically transcended.*

Adidam is a universally applicable Way of life.
Adidam is for those who will choose it, and whose
   hearts and intelligence fully respond to Me and My
   Offering.
Adidam is a Great Revelation, and It is to be freely and
   openly communicated to all.

—ADI DA SAMRAJ

WORLDWIDE CENTERS OF ADIDAM

Adidam has established centers in many locations around the world, offering courses, seminars, and retreats for the public as well as formal devotees of Avatar Adi Da. The listings below provide contact information for you to find out more about Avatar Adi Da and Adidam.

Americas
12040 N. Seigler Road
Middletown, CA
95461 USA
1-707-928-4936

Australia
P.O. Box 244
Kew 3101
Victoria
1800 ADIDAM
(1800-234-326)

Europe-Africa
Annendaalderweg 10
6105 AT Maria Hoop
The Netherlands
31 (0)20 468 1442

India
F-168 Shree Love-Ananda Marg
Rampath, Shyam Nagar Extn.
Jaipur - 302 019, India
91 (141) 2293080

Pacific-Asia
12 Seibel Road
Henderson
Auckland 0614
New Zealand
64-9-838-9114

The United Kingdom
uk@adidam.org
0845-330-1008

ONLINE RESOURCES

Adidam website: www.adidam.org

E-mail: correspondence@adidam.org

Publications: www.dawnhorsepress.com

Courses: www.adidamacademy.org

Adidam centers and events: www.adidam.org/events.html

Visual art of Adi Da Samraj: www.adidabiennale.org
www.daplastique.com

Literary and theatrical art of Adi Da Samraj: www.mummerybook.org

INDEX